The Grandeur Of Om

Mandukya Upanishad - A Meditative Approach

Dr. Tejaswi Katravulapally

Contact me at
e-mail: ardentdisciple7@gmail.com
Phone: +919381195828
Whatsapp: +353892254459

To my Guru who is ever present in every beat of my heart - Master E K

From the beauty of dreams, arises a Hope

Hope causes a spark of determination

The fire of Determination is fueled by constant contemplation

Slowly, our actions incline towards the goal, but

The path filled with many obstacles test the strength of the fire

And thus one needs to have Faith in his dreams and strengths !!

He is the happiest and blessed who fulfills his dreams, with a positive hope crossing the ocean of obstacles having strong determination and faith !

DR. TEJASWI KATRAVULAPALLY

Contents

Title Page

Copyright

Dedication

Epigraph

Preface

Introduction 1

Peace Invocation 6

Aphorisms 9

1. Introduction To Om 10

2. Universal Self & Individual Self 21

3. The Being In The Universe - Vaiśvānara 30

4. The Inner Brilliance - Taijasa 43

5. The Conscious Intelligence - Prajña 51

6. Prajña As The Light Of Gāyatrī 60

7. The core philosophy of Non-Dualism - Advaita 65

8. The Threefold Division Of Om: A-U-M 73
9. Syllable A - Vaiśvānara 80
10. Syllable U - Taijasa 85
11. Syllable M - Prajña 91
12. The Divine Essence Of Om Is Brahman 96
Transliteration Scheme 101
Acknowledgement 105
About The Author 107
Books By This Author 109

Preface

The Vēdic lore is a vast forest occupied by the trees of eternal wisdom having many branches bearing the fruits of self realisation. When one tries to enter such a forest with bare hands, they are destined to be lost in its confusing intertwined nexus. If they try to forcefully cut the obstructing nexus with the axe of personal prejudice, then they would break the hidden harmony of links which connect the many trees as the ONE forest. This kills the very purpose of the existence of the forest which is to offer us its fruits. Then what do we do? Instead of using the axe of personal prejudice or bare hands, the explorer needs to get the torch of the intuition of the seers which shines the many paths that direct towards the central tree of wisdom. Then it is easy to just tread carefully and reach the required tree bearing the desired fruit.

Vēda, being one of the oldest compendiums of human wisdom, is always looked upon with reverence. One of my books titled *Journey through the Vēdic thought - An exploration of Puruṣa Sūktaṃ*, gives an in-depth exposition as to what Vēda means. **Vēda** is the wisdom that **ALL-IS-ONE**. **Vēdic-text** is a literary form that expresses this wisdom in multiple ways. The Vēda was expressed in the literary (or oratory) form during the times when such an art was flourishing as a natural trait. But with the course of time, the original art of expressing the intuitive idea and grasping the same was lost, and hence there arose a present need to induce humanity into a similar scheme of things which is far superior than the present day linear approaches. To train in such a way of life, one should atleast have an idea as to what Vēda is trying to say. To cater to this need, three categories of wisdom sprung forth from the heart of the seers. They were ***Brāhmaṇās, Āraṇyakās and Upaniṣads***.

Amongst these, the most direct yet profound approach is taken by the Upaniṣads. *Upanishad means that which takes us nearer*. Nearer to what? Nearer to the Vēda. So, the torch that I was speaking about is the Upaniṣadic torch. There are many Upaniṣads, just like there are many torch lights. One torch may be brighter and bigger than the other but they all serve the same purpose of shedding light, do they not? Similarly, the many Upaniṣads serve the same purpose of breaking the limits of our restrictive domains of understanding and relaxing the prejudiced constraints by expanding our contemplative horizons. Only then can we purely grasp what Vēda is trying to say and only then can we put into practice the right way of life - the harmonious one, as indicated and lived by the seers.

Amongst the many Upaniṣads, **Māṇḍūkya Upaniṣad (MU)** is the shortest. There is a proverb in Telugu -

“Piṭṭa Konchaṃ Kūta Ghanaṃ”, meaning - Even the smallest bird has a loud voice. Similarly, the seemingly smallest Upaniṣad shouts out loud the grandeur of Vēdic lore. MU is an exposition of the concept of Ōṃ We all know that the Vēdic text is either in a prose or in a poetry form. Irrespective of these forms, every part of the Vēdic utterance starts with an invocation of the sound of Ōṃ . So, naturally Ōṃ must be very important. In the form of 12 aphorisms, the quintessence of Ōṃ is given in this MU. Understanding this, helps us bring a meaning to the invocation of Ōṃ in our daily life.

This work is dedicated to the Ōṃ itself which is very the ONE-IN-ALL.

Tejaswi Katravulapally
ardentdisciple7@gmail.com

Introduction

Māṇḍūkya Upaniṣad (MU) belongs to the Atharvaṇa Vēda. Atharvaṇa Vēda is the fourth Vēda which is said to act as the lower jaw while the three other Vēdas act as the upper jaw of the Lord Omnipresent. The role of the lower jaw is to externalise the WORD or the intent within. The intent within the Omnipresent is uttered forth in an articulated i.e., structured or organised manner by Atahrvaṇa Vēda. So, an Upaniṣad belonging to such a Vēda acts as a guiding manual to practically set forth the guiding principles of the Vēda into daily practice. The same can be seen in MU as you go through the following pages.

MU consists of 12 aphorisms. In just these 12 aphorisms, the whole story and the synthesis of understanding the concept of Ōṃ is given. One should ask why just 12 aphorisms? Why not 13 or 10 or 100? A number constraint often suggests the nature of exploration that is contained in the given context. For example, the epic Mahābhārata has number

18 repeating in the form of 18 groups of armies, 18 days of war, written in 18 cantos, etc. In fact, the original name of the main text of the Mahābhāratha is **Jaya** which is numerically equivalent to the number **18** by the law of numerical-correspondences (**Ja = 8, Ya = 1** and the rule of reading numbers leftward (*aṃkānāṃ vāmatō gatiḥ*) is to be applied i.e., 81 --> 18). So, understanding number 18 helps in decoding the wisdom of the epic of the Mahābhāratha.

Similarly, the number in our present context is **12**. It is the number that determines two things - Time and Space. Time aspect is determined via the 12 months causing a solar year-cycle in which sprouts the variegated life forms on the Earth. In the Purāṇās, we find the number 12 associated with the Dvādaśa Aādityās or 12 SUNs of which our SUN is one. And SUN is indeed the ruler of TIME. Here, the perception of time is meant rather than the time itself. So, the number 12 is definitely associated with our ability to understand time and its effects on us via the SUN-principle. Also, the Vēda says "***Yajñō vai saṃvatsaraḥ***" which means, the year-cycle is verily a Yajña. Therefore, the number 12 is related to the Yajña-Puruṣa or the in-dweller of the solar Yajña, by whom the 12 month cycle is ever rotating. On the other hand, 12 zodiacal divisions that spread across the vast canopy of space around the equatorial belt surrounding the Earth is the cause of evolutionary patterns on the Earth as per the Astrological key (***Nakṣatrāṇi Rūpaṃ*** says the Rig Vēda, meaning the constellation of stars constitute the visible aspect of

Omnipresent Puruṣa). This covers the spatial aspect of number 12 i.e., the spread of the principle of ZODIAC in space.

Both put together suggest that the SUN traversing through the 12 Zodiac signs kindles and steers the journeys of the life forms on the Earth, on the background of the space-time matrix. The source of all this glory is actually attributed to the inner-SUN (**sūryāntarvarti**) who is the cause of all the SUNs and the Zodiacs or for that matter the whole cosmos. So, the number 12 is attributed to the visible forms via the above associations but to the invisible via the permeating principle of the Inner-SUN. *This all pervading, all encompassing and ever existing almighty is what this MU names as the **inaudible*** Ōṃ *while the splendours of the manifested creation is named as the **audible*** Ōṃ.

MU is more an instruction manual than a reference book. MU itself says that the true Ōṃ is incomprehensible and inexplicable. Then what is the use of giving tenets pertaining to such an unknowable entity? This clearly suggests that the aphorisms given in MU are more of instructional type than information type. They teach us the true way of meditation which is expounded by many Vēdic seers. This consists of uttering the AUM aloud and hearing it. While uttering and hearing, the tenets as proposed in MU need to be run on the background which help us a lot in shaping the unknown journey of our inner meditation. It takes us from the gross to the subtle or from the outer world to the innermost world. A mere glance at MU would put all sorts of doubts in the heads of scholars. But when each aphorism is contemplated and synthesised as an active part of our life, a true aspirant will start to awaken his intuition and awareness into the real subject of the Upaniṣad and the brilliance of Ōṃ starts to shine from within.

To give a clear picture as to what MU is trying to instruct us, I have chosen to give two examples of meditation:

1. Meditating on the different gradations of consciousness which manifested as different kingdoms such as mineral, plant, animal and human.

2. Meditating on the utterance of a word by us which again occurs in four stages namely impulse to speak, hazy idea, mental blueprint and the physically uttered word.

I have related all the tenets of Ōṃ as proposed by MU to the aforementioned two examples. This helps an aspirant to efficiently grab the abstract and difficult notions that are systematically arranged in the MU. Where necessary many correlations have been shown between different branches of wisdom such as Purāṇās, Itihāsās, Vēdānta, Tantra, Śrī Vidyā, etc. This holistic and harmonious approach is hoped to shed light not only on the present MU but also on the other branches of wisdom which helps a sincere aspirant in understanding the truth that the many branches of wisdom are but multiple limbs of the one GOD who is the content of all such wisdom branches.

A key point to note before proceeding is the usage of two kinds of "**I am**" and "**I AM**" in my exploration. The "I am" corresponds to the individual self. It is the same when we use the statements like "I am so and so" or "I am enjoying this" etc. This is what everyone of us point towards ourselves and indicate as ourselves. The "I AM" corresponds to the Universal self - the GOD in all. No one can utter or know this but everyone has a potential to become this.

Let us now proceed to understand the Upaniṣad from a perspective of a vēdic seer.

Peace Invocation

Most of the Vēdic mantras have a peace invocation before and after the main text. Generally our mind is always in a constant disturbance. A disturbed mind cannot clearly perceive the truth. For example, consider someone holding a rope in the dark. They might mistake it to a snake and sweat in terror. Such is the delusive state of a disturbed mind. Therefore, to calm the mind and let us perceive the truth in all its glory, a peace invocation is uttered before the main text of the Vēda. This upaniṣad also has one such invocation. It is as follows,

Ōṃ! bhadraṃ karṇēbhiḥ śṛṇuyāma devā
bhadram paśyēmākṣhabhiryajatrāḥ |
sthirairaṃgaistuṣṭuvāṃsastanūbhir vyaśēma
dēvahitaṃ yadāyuḥ ||
svasti na indrō vriddhaśravāh svasti naḥ pūṣā
viśvavēdāḥ |
svasti nastārkṣhyō ariṣṭanēmiḥ svasti nō
bṛhaspatirdadhātu ||
Ōṃ śāntiḥ śāntiḥ śāntiḥ !

Import: Ōṃ *Oh dēvās, may we hear only what is aus-*

picious. Oh the lord of sacrifices, may we see only that which is auspicious. May we enter into long stable life forms with help of gods. Oh Indra - the glorious, Pūṣā - the wisest, Tarshkya - the evil dispeller and Bṛhaspati, may you all bestow unto us the well being".

Thus, we pray to the subtle and inner faculties of our human existence (Indra, Pūsha, etc.) as well as to the cosmic faculties like Dēvās for a seamless and uninterrupted evolution into the light of wisdom pearls of the divine ŌṂ!

Aphorisms

1. Introduction To Ōm

Ōṃ Ityētadakṣaraṃidaṃ Sarvaṃ Tasyopavyākhyānaṃ Bhūtaṃ Bhavad Bhaviṣyaditi Sarvamōṃkāra Ēva Yaccānyat Trikālātītaṃ Tadapyōṃkāra Eva

Word To Word Meaning:

Ōṃ = *AUM;* **Itiyētat** = *this Ōṃ;* **Akṣaraṃ** = *indestructible or syllable;* **Idaṃ Sarvaṃ** = *all this/that;* **Tasya** = *of this;* **Upavyākhyānaṃ** = *an exposition;* **Bhūtaṃ** = *past;* **Bhavad** = *present;* **Bhaviṣyad** = *future;* **iti** = *in this manner;* **Sarvaṃ** = *all;* **Ōṃkāra** = *AUM;* **Ēva** = *indeed;* **Yat +Ca+Anyat** = *that which is different;* **Trikāla + Atītaṃ** = *Beyond the three modes of time;* **Tat** = *that;* **Api** = *also;* **Ōṃkāra** = *AUM;* **Ēva** = *indeed.*

Import:

The AUM is an indestructible entity or a syllable. All that we say as "this or that" are indeed AUM. The three modes of time that we experience as past, present and future as well as the other aspect of time which is beyond this trio are indeed AUM. This is an exposition of AUM.

Explanation:

For the purposes which will be clear later on, let us denote Ōṃ by AUM. If you have observed closely, the peace invocation started with AUM. In fact any Vēdic mantra starts with AUM. As mentioned before, a peace invocation occurs before and after the main text of the Vēda. What is the Upaniṣad about? It is about AUM. Then, how can one utter AUM even before knowing what it is? This is to suggest that to understand AUM the first step of the approach is not analytical in nature but is synthesis in nature i.e., you need to utter AUM in a meditative way so as to experience its LIGHT rather than read pages and pages about AUM. You need to first after AUM before even embarking on a journey to understand it. This gives a vague experience at first. To polish this experience, the present Upaniṣad embarks on an epic journey to reveal the subtleties associated with this AUM. The former is primary and the latter is secondary. When you are hungry, what is the use of studying the biology of digestion and chemistry of cooking? You have to first go to the kitchen, cook and then eat. This gives a vague feeling of satisfaction. But when you know the process of digestion and art of cooking, your experience of satiation shapes to perfection. The same is true here. Therefore, reading the Upaniṣad cannot alone make us understand the nature of AUM. It is the simultaneous linking of its tenets along with a meditative utterance that help us unveil the wealth of wisdom pertaining to AUM within us.

When I say meditative utterance, I mean a state of utterance where the utterer, uttered and the process of utterance collapse into unit existence. In parlance of Tantric language, this is called the collapse of the triangle into the mother Bindu (point of infinite existence).

The first set of principles to be understood about

AUM are given by the first aphorism. The key points of its proclamation are as follows

AUM is imperishable - Akṣaraṃ

What is Akṣaraṃ? Literally it has two meanings: One, that it is imperishable and two, that it is a syllable (the Sanskrit syllables from A to Kṣa). Do syllables exist in us? If so, when our bodies perish, the syllables too should perish along with it. Do they vanish so? No! Even when we are not there, others are able to speak the syllables. That means, syllables are imperishable. You may say that when we erase the letters on black-board, we are eliminating them, aren't we?. But that which is written on a board is a symbol for a syllable and not syllable itself. Your name is a symbol to indicate you but not yourself, right? A symbol only acts as a trigger to kindle the true syllable in us. In fact, the principle of syllable works through us and that is the reason why everyone of us are able to reproduce infinite such syllables every second with our thought, word or deed!

The essence is that the common thread of meaning associated with the word Akṣaraṃ is **imperishability**. It seems that AUM is imperishable in nature. If closely observed, when we do not think or utter syllables, they seem to be resting somewhere in poise. So they have a state of alternating existence with respect to our perception. That means the syllables are not constant entities and are not totally imperishable as we thought! They can be said to be relatively perished - relative to our state of consciousness. But, after the period of rest, one is able to bring forth the syllables from something. If that something had a state of rest or the aspect to perish, we wouldn't have been able to squeeze out the syllables as much as we desired. That something is the imperishable AUM that is being spoken here. AUM forms the basis for syllables and acts as a vault of syllables for our purposes. Syllables can not describe AUM but AUM contains and sustains all the syllables. That is why the dual meaning word - **Akṣaraṃ** is used to indicate AUM so as to suggest that it is imperishable as well as that it is the source of all syllables (and hence the basis of all the meanings of our words, sentences, expressions, interactions and our very existence). This is the reason why any mantra starts with AUM. A mantra is nothing but an experience of a seer encoded in a combination of syllables, and the source of experience is verily AUM!

AUM is ALL

It is being said that AUM is **ALL** or **Sarvaṃ**. The word "All" constitutes people, birds, plants, organisms, mountains, sand, planets, moons, etc. How can AUM be all these? No Vēda or its explanation-manual Upaniṣad can be directly understood as a single piece of text. It needs to be understood in the light of other scriptures. This is because each scripture is only a fragment of the absolute TRUTH and only when understood holistically, does all these fragments add up to give a harmonious picture of their contents.

It is said in Puruṣa Sūkta (refer to my book **Journey through the Vēdic thought - an exploration of Puruṣa Sūkta**, available via Amazon and Notion Press) that the life and life-less beings originate from the Omnipresent lord and it is stated in the hymns related to goddess Saraswathi that the universe originates as the WORD of God. This line of thought is also found in other world scriptures. Take the old testament for example. The old testament (John 1:1) suggests the same thing in a cryptic language - "*In the beginning was the Word, and the Word was with God, and the Word was God*". What do such statements try to say? They are trying to suggest to us that the visible universe is a structured sentence made up of words (beings and entities) which are uttered forth by the Omnipresent lord called GOD. From the first principle that AUM is the basis for any word (physical or non-physical) it can be deduced that if the "ALL" is the result of words, then AUM must also be the basis for the word uttered by GOD. Therefore, it is stated that **AUM is ALL** - a single capsule statement indeed!

AUM is the whole cosmos

Cosmos is, as pointed above, a structured sentence of the words uttered forth by GOD. Therefore, Cosmos is also verily Ōṃ! There is a branch of science by the name Cymatics. It proposes a theory that the Universe originates from primordial sound. To prove this, it takes a vibrating plate and sprinkles very fine particles (of sand or grains) on it. As the frequency of the vibrating plate changes, the randomly spread particles form peculiar patterns. In a similar way this branch of science suggests that at the moment of origin of the Universe, a great primordial sound imprinted the matter with plethora of structure and sub-structures. This resulted in the many forms. In the later aphorisms of MU we will see that Ōṃ is nothing but the primordial sound (Nāda and beyond). Therefore, the theory proposed by the Cymatics and the point put forward in the present aphorism are synonymous i.e., Ōṃ is indeed the whole cosmos!

AUM can be characterized by time as past, present and future

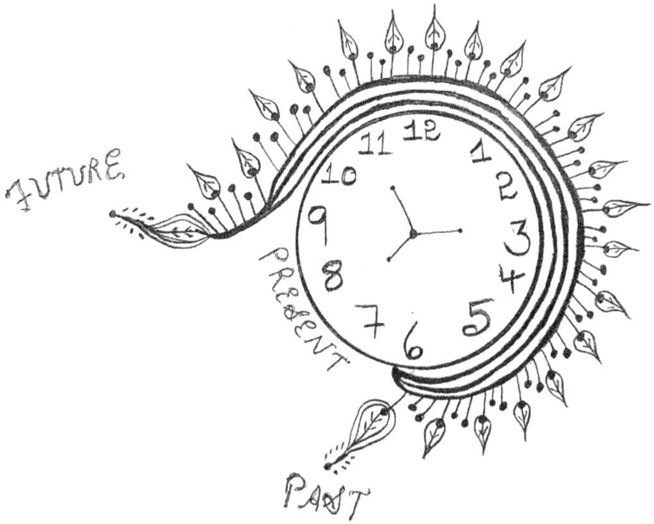

Time is a peculiar and enigmatic element that can never be fully understood. What is time? Is it your clock? A clock can only indicate time but not time itself. So, no one actually knows what time is. But everyone behaves and executes their life only through time. Even a flap of an eyelid has a duration of time as its periodicity. Everyone experiences time as succession events. But no one truly knows what time is. It is being said that time is nothing but AUM and can be understood as the three-fold division of past-present-future.

Previously, the space-aspect had been described i.e.,

the equivalence of AUM to the cosmos, ALL, etc. That is a partial truth. Now, the equivalence of AUM and time aspect is being described. This is also a partial truth. But when combined, we understand that AUM is the space-time matrix itself. What is special about the space-time matrix? It is the web of threads which weave the creation's existence or dissolution as a garment to the Lord omnipresent! Other than the space and time can we experience anything else? No! The thoughts, dreams, feelings, opinions, happiness, sadness, our jobs, pass times, etc., exist only in space and run in time. We should remember that when we speak of "space", actually three kinds of space are being indicated, namely, the **Ghanākāśa/ Bhūtākāśa** (the outer physical space which also permeates through our body), the **Cittākāśa** (the mental space where thoughts arise) and **Daharākāśa** (the space of heart which pulsates the life element - it is often called the residence of GOD in us). Therefore, it is stated that AUM is the very fabric of this Universe as well as that it is verily the Universe in such a fabric.

AUM is beyond time

All the aforementioned aspects relate to our wake-state i.e., our perceivable state. Space-time, things, life, sentences, etc., relate to our awareness. What about the sleep? When we sleep, do we perceive any of these? If we do, how can it be called a sleeping state? If we ask a sleeping person "Are you asleep" and if they answer "Yes, I am sleeping", are they really sleeping? No! Sleep state is where the "I am" in the statement "I am sleeping" does not exist. Where does it go? Or, who exists when we are actually asleep, if not ourselves? Scriptures suggest that there are two selves in us - individual self and Universal self. The individual self sleeps and wakes but the Universal self always exists (there is no dual principal of wake/sleep to it). When the individual self is awake, it has its own experiences on the background of the universal self. But when it sleeps, it is dissolved into the background. A perfect example to think about this is the formation of an ice-berg and its dissolution in water. Ice-berg is the individual self and the ocean is the Universal self.

Now this Universal self cannot be constrained by time whereas the individual self is. MU is saying that the beyondness of time attributed to the Universal self is nothing but AUM. Earlier it was stated that the cosmos is AUM. What happens to AUM when cosmos perishes? AUM was already said to be imperishable, but we all know cosmos would perish at one point time or the other (draw parallel to our sleep/wake and life/death aspects to the birth/death of cosmos). Then, how can cosmos be AUM? Here, relating to the time-aspect of AUM as well, we understand that cosmos does not only mean the visible cosmos but also the cosmos's periodical occurrence. Vēdic scriptures suggest a cyclicity for creation. For the cosmos to periodically originate and merge, there should be a constant principle (like an ocean of existence) working as the background source. This should be beyond time because time also originates from it. Such a beyondness is actually AUM.

So the last principle suggests that the root source of all is a constant principle beyond space and time - the ocean of Omnipresence!

No once again look through all the key points proposed by MU. At first sight the exploration may seem paradoxical or one point negating the other. But in its deeper synthesis it suggests that the first aphorism of MU has taken us step by step from ***what we understand as AUM to what we need to experience as AUM***. These are key instructions to meditate upon AUM. First medictate AUM as a visible universe, then as the time, then as the fabric of space-time and then as something that is beyond time - which in essence is verily ourselves (from individual "I am" to the universal "I AM")!

∞∞∞

2. Universal Self & Individual Self

Sarvaṃ Hyētad Brahmāyamātmā Brahma Sōyamātmā Catuṣpāt

Word To Word Meaning:

Sarvaṃ = *all;* **Hi** = *surely;* **Ētad** = *this;* **Brahma** = *Brahman (GOD);* **Ayaṃ** = *this;* **Ātmā** = *soul;* **Saḥ** = *he;* **Ayaṃ** = *this;* **Ātmā** = *soul;* **Catuṣ** = *four;* **Pāt** = *one fourth parts.*

Import:

All this is surely Brahman (GOD). This soul is also Brahman. He, the soul (or Brahman), is said to be having four parts.

Explanation:

In this aphorism, the concept of "BRAHMAN" and "Ātma (self)"is brought into picture. The **Brahma** here is different from **Brahma** of Purāṇās (like Bhāgavataṃ or Viṣṇu purāṇa, etc.) The latter denotes the creation aspect presided by creator-Brahma who is one among the trinity-godheads of creation, the other two being Viṣṇu (sustenance) and Rudra (dissolution). But the "Brahma" here denotes the supreme GOD above ALL. It is equivalent to the **Brahman** of Vēdānta. For clarity sake, let us use the word Brahman instead of Brahma, in our explorations, to represent the Universal consciousness. **Ātma** is the individualised soul-consciousness which seems to have its own existence separate from that of Brahma. Remember the ice-berg example given in the previous aphorism? Ātma is such an iceberg floating in the ocean of Brahman.

The key points brought to our attention by the present sentence are as follows:

- **All that you perceive is Brahman.**
- **What you call as "this or that or He or Ātma (self)" is verily Brahman.**
- **There are four-paths to this self or the self is four-fold.**

Previously it was stated that AUM is ALL and now it is being stated that ALL is Brahman. Therefore by transitive property, the seers are suggesting that **AUM is verily BRAHMAN.**

This Brahman, owing to some divine drama (Māya, as it is often termed in Vēdānta), gives rise to the whole cosmos filled with many Ātmās. But it is stated that what you call as "This" or "That" or

"Ātmā" or "He" is nothing but Brahman. How can this be? Imagine the ocean again and along with it, some ripples over it. Though ripples occur in the ocean, the ocean is still an ocean. We can not imagine ripples independent of the ocean but we can imagine the ocean without ripples! Similarly, Brahman without Ātma can exist (during Praḷaya/divine dissolution) but an Ātma or any entity in the Universe can never exist without Brahman.

There is another hidden mantra in this aphorism - the **Haṃsa mantra (Swan mantra)** or **Sōhaṃ mantra (Breathing mantra)**. It is said that Saḥ+Ātma is Brahman. Ātma means Ahaṃ (self). The hidden import is Saḥ+Ahaṃ is Brahman. Saḥ+Ahaṃ becomes Sōhaṃ and therefore Sōhaṃ is Brahman. But we already saw that Brahman is AUM and therefore Sōham is AUM. Can you see AUM (Ōṃ) in Sōham? You will see if you understand the pretext of the nature of syllables in Sanskrit.

There are two categories of syllables: **Vowels** (Śakti) and **Consonants** (Śiva) in the Sanskrit alphabet. Consonants cannot be uttered without the help of Vowels. But vowels can be uttered without the help of consonants. Try to utter the sanskrit syllable "K (क्)" and compare it with the utterance of "Ka (क)" or "Kā (का)". To utter just the consonant "K" your vocals came together but the air (Prāṇā) did not flow through it. So, it did not utterforth as a sustained audible sound. But when you try to utter "Ka" or "Kā" you could utter the sound of "K" out of your vocals due to the free flow of Prāṇa in it. Therefore, the vowels give life to the consonants and they stand as the permeating agents to utterforth a syllable. The same is true in terms of WORD of creation as well. That is why in the first stanza of Saundarya Laharī, Sri Śankarācārya says that when Śakti doesn't cooperate, Śiva stays still like a corpse i.e., if not for energy, the dynamism of the Universe collapses into static slumber. Using this knowledge, apply the concepts to the word Sōhaṃ. The consonants in the word Sōhaṃ are "Sa" and "Ha". When you remove them, the underlying lifegiving vowels are "Ō" and "ṃ". Combining these we obtain "Ōṃ", denoted as AUM. This is nothing but the underlying Nāda (inaudible sound) of the inner-self which breathes in "Sa" (sound of inhalation at the tip of the nose) and exhales "Ha" (sound of exhalation at the beginning of the throat) through our breath. That is why Sōhaṃ is also linked to breathing meditation. All these key points are artistically hidden in this aphorism.

MU is saying that the way Brahman creates the Ātma is through 4 stages. This is intimately connected to the "Catvāri Vāk" concept of Saraswati Sūkta which suggests that the WORD uttered by the GOD occurs in four stages, namely Parā Vāk, Paśyaṃtī Vāk, Madhyamā Vāk and Vaikharī Vāk. These stages can be better understood with a small example (in reverse order i.e., from physical to subtle).

- **Vaikharī Vāk:** Let us utter a statement "I like apples". To produce this sound, we used vocals, lips, teeth and tongue. Whatever we used, the effect is the utterance of a complete sentence aloud. The stage of this physical sentence is associated with the fourth or the final stage of the Brahman becoming Ātma i.e., Ātmās being formed.
- **Madhyamā Vāk:** Now, to have uttered the above sentence, we should have had the same statement as a thought (say like a *mental blueprint*) in our mind so that the brain could give the appropriate signals to the respective organs so as to produce the needed utterance. This stage of mental blueprint of the sentence is associated with the mental blueprint of the plan pertaining to the creation of Ātma in Brahman's mind.
- **Paśyaṃtī Vāk:** To have such a mental blueprint, we must have had a vague idea in our mind as to what to speak - "should I say I like apples or I like oranges", etc., without which a concrete mental blueprint wouldn't have been formed at all. This stage of cloudy idea of the sentence is as-

sociated with the Brahman's pre-planning stage of the Ātma.

- **Parā Vāk:** Even before getting a vague idea as to what to speak, we require an impulse/inspiration to speak. Otherwise, we won't speak at all in the first place, instead we would be doing whatever we were doing prior to the utterance. Such a stage of generation of impulse to speak is associated with the impulses to create that arise in Brahman which forms the starting point for creation to arise from the state of dissolution (pre-existing state).

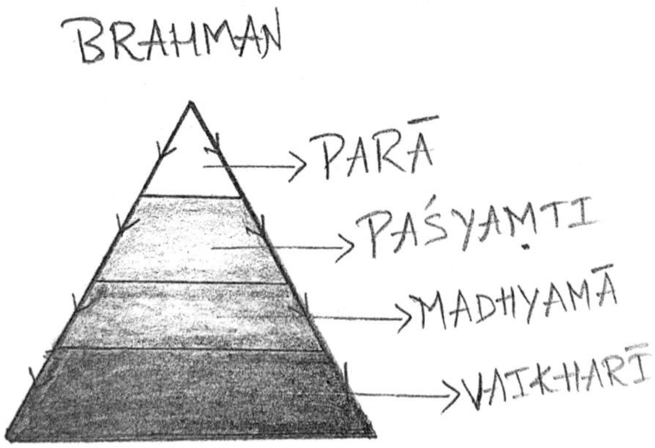

This is what is actually meant by the 4-staged creation of Ātma by Brahman.

The same can be understood as the 4-fold existence of Ātma in Brahman which is associated with its degree of consciousness. Starting from gross to subtle,

- **Mineral Kingdom - Suṣupti state:** The Ātma in this state has a consciousness in its deep sleeping state. All the physical matter such as minerals, stones, planetary bodies, their cores, etc., come under this category. This is the grossest state of Ātma's existence.
- **Plant Kingdom - Svapna state:** Here the consciousness exists in a dreamy state. Plants, crops, trees, some microorganisms, etc., belong to this category. The Ātma in these beings is hazy in its awareness. For example, they feel "pain" as something that is spread all over their body rather than having a localized sensation at a particular location. That is why Sri Ramana Maharshi used to say that we should pluck a fruit or a leaf from a tree only gently and in a loving manner.
- **Animal Kingdom - Jāgṛt State-lower:** Here consciousness is awoken and is aware of all its surroundings. But the meaning of its own existence is far from its reach. Questions such as "Who am I" do not even arise in this state. But their life is driven by basic instincts such as fear, hunger, sexual desires, etc. All the animals, insects, birds, etc., belong to this category.
- **Human Kingdom - Jāgṛt state-higher:** Here, the

consciousness is not only aware of surroundings but also aware of its own self. It can comprehend the question "Who am I" and contemplate on it. It has the power of discrimination - the capacity to choose one (right) from the other (wrong). Humans belong to this category.

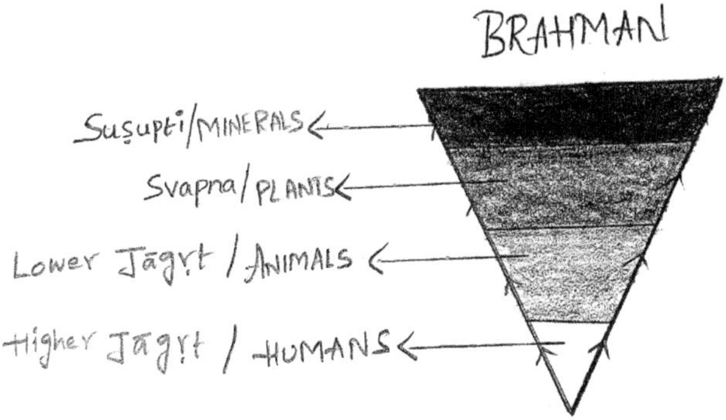

But there is a permeating kingdom in all the aforementioned 4 kingdoms. It's called **The Kingdom of GOD - Omnipresent**! When consciousness awakens to such a stage where there is only ONE and no dual aspect to it, it is said to have reached the kingdom of GOD and in the scriptures it is called "**Turīya state**". In the previous parlance of the Vāk, the kingdom of GOD is the ever existing medium in which the Parā Vāk impulse originates. Therefore, the default kingdom of GOD (including the medium of parā vāk) is ever existing and it is in this the play of 4-fold-ness occurs. The Vāk symbolizes the descent of Brahman into gross creation whereas the kingdoms and degree of awareness indicate the way of ascent of the individual soul-consciousness to rise into the Universal consciousness-Brahman.

So, when it is said that Ātma is four-fold in its existence, this is what is meant. The coming aphorisms will clarify the division in a much more scientific way. But for now, take the above four stages as going from gross to subtle in their awareness of the Ātma's equivalence with Brahman.

∞∞∞

3. The Being In The Universe - Vaiśvānara

Jāgaritasthānō Bahiṣprajñaḥ Saptāṃga Ēkōnaviṃśatimukhaḥ Sthūlabhug Vaiśvānaraḥ Prathamaḥ Pādaḥ

Word To Word Meaning:

Jāgaritasthānaḥ = *the realm of existence is wide awake;* **Bahiṣ+Prajñaḥ** = *awareness that is outward;* **Sapta +Aṃgaḥ** = *having 7 limbs;* **Ēkōnaviṃśati** = *19;* **Mukhaḥ** = *mouths (or doors);* **Sthūlabhuk** = *that which enjoys the gross world;* **Vaiśvānaraḥ** = *the being in the Universe;* **prathama** = *first;* **pādaḥ** = *part.*

Import:

*The first part (of Ātmā) is named Vaiśvānaraḥ (the **being** in the Universe). The realm of its existence is a wide awoken state. Its awareness is always turned outward. It has 7 limbs and 19 mouths (or doors) and enjoys the* *gross world.*

Explanation:

The first of the 4-folds of the self or 4-stages of descent of the Universal self into the individualised self is now being described. Let us call these four folds or four stages of descent as "parts". In Sanskrit "Pāda" means one-fourth of something i.e., a quarter part. The upcoming four parts make a whole UNIT and hence should be understood only as a whole. By looking at your hand alone, can I say something about you? No! Similarly the one-quarter wisdom alone cannot speak about the whole process pertaining to the four-fold division of the scheme of descent of creation or evolution of the soul. Therefore each of the one-fourth pāda, representing each step in the evolution/descent of the self, though is very important, is not to be independently studied.

In this and in the forthcoming aphorisms, the description of the parts is given from gross to subtle. One may ask as to why this reverse order had been chosen. It is for our comprehension. We may not comprehend the abstract Brhman in the first attempt itself. Therefore, our awareness is taken step by step for the outer to inner self and that is why the first pāda is going to speak about the last stage of creation or the last fold of the self.

The first fold is called Vaiśvānara

Here etymologically speaking, the word Vaiśvānara indicates the prototype of the Universal self. The word originates from **Viśva** and **Nara**. Viśva indicates Universal and Nara indicates an individualised self. Infact, Nara and Nārāyaṇa are intimately linked. In the Mahābhārata, Arjuna was symbolic to Nara whereas Lord Krishna was symbolic to Nārāyaṇa. Nāra means divine waters in the Vēda. These are not the physical waters but the waters that originate LIFE. The vacuum of space that we perceive as nothing is said to be filled by this Nāra according to the Vēda. When there is a ripple in this Nāra, there will be a birth of creation. These ripples may be called Quantum Fluctuations, in a gross sense, which modern physics proposes as that which fills through the apparent vacuum of space. A movement in these waters of life is called "Ayana" and hence Nāra +Ayana = Nārāyaṇa is the one in whom the creations sprouts due to the ripples/movements in the waters of slumbering life. In purāṇās, this whole symbolism is depicted as Lord Viṣṇu sleeping on the bed of ocean from whose navel sprouts a lotus in which wakes Brahma the creator.

The elements of his prototype in his creation are called Nara. When you make an earthen pot from clay, the contents of the pot are nothing but the atoms of clay, except that there is a difference of state of its being. Clay can be moulded but a pot cannot be moulded. In essence, both are the same and when the pot is decomposed into its finer elements, the atoms of the clay are restored to their original state. The same happens when the creator consciousness Brahma creates a creation. Before him was Nārāyaṇa alone and after his birth also is Nārāyaṇa. Therefore to create, the only material he has is Nārāyaṇa. Thus, the creation he makes is filled and permeated by this Nārāyaṇa only - this is the reason for Lord's nature of Omnipresence. The same symbolism is seen in Puruṣa Sūktaṃ of the Rig Vēda where it is said that the dēvās take the first puruṣa as a sacrifice in the Yajña of creation (yat puruṣēṇa haviṣā .....). So, the same symbolism keeps on repeating no matter the scripture.

Therefore, Nara is same as Nārāyaṇa in all the essence except for his state of being. When that state of being is also refined to mimic Nārāyaṇa, the Nara becomes one with Viṣvaṃ (cosmos) and hence is called Vaiśvānara. Therefore, Vaiśvānara is that concept of Nara which fills the whole Universe. In Āyurvēda he is a form of Agni - the fire. Therefore Vaiśvānara can be called "**The fire of LIFE**". This is what is the summary of the first pāda.

It is the wakeful consciousness and It is awakened outward

What is its nature of this Vaiśvānara who is the grossest manifestation of the Lord Omnipresent? It seems he is fully awake - Jāgṛt. Now correlate the previously discussed stages of **Vāk** and different **kingdoms**. We see that Vaiśvānara is indicated by the Human and animal kingdoms (higher and lower awakened stages of consciousness) as well as the Vaikharī and Madhyamā Vāk (physically uttered word and its exact mental blueprint). The aspect of outward awakening implies either the formation of a physical/mental word which is uttered forth outward or the awareness of consciousness to recognize itself and its fellow individualised beings as separate entities.

This is the main drama of the puzzling nature of God. The seers say that ***he separates himself out of himself and then tries to unite with himself to experience himself***! To understand this, an example may be given. Consider sugar crystals and your tongue. As long as sugar is separate from your tongue, there is no experience of sweetness. But only when the sugar contacts the tongue and mixes with the saliva, we experience its sweetness. Can tongue taste itself? Can sugar taste itself? No! The experience obtained when two seemingly separate entities dissolve as one entity is what is the purpose of God's drama of creation. Therefore the prathama pāda indicates the final step of this separation of self or gross condensation of consciousness which needs to be restored to its past glory. This union is called **Yōga** in the scriptures!

It has 7 limbs

It seems that Vaiśvānara has 7 limbs! How so? Consider the human/animal bodily constitution. Āyurvēda suggests that the physical body is comprised of 7 main Dhātūs or tissues

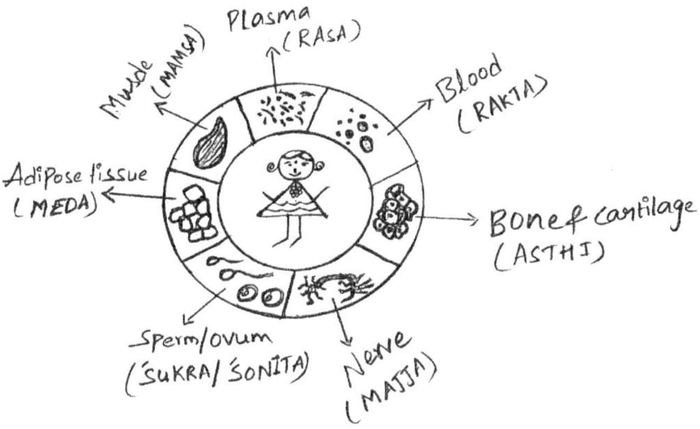

1. ***Rasa*** (plasma fluids)
2. ***Rakta*** (blood)
3. ***Mamsa*** (muscle)
4. ***Meda*** (adipose tissue)
5. ***Asthi*** (bones and Cartilage)
6. ***Majja*** (bone marrow)
7. ***Shukra*** (reproductive elements)

As already pointed out earlier Vaiśvānara is correlated to animal/human kingdom. The 7 dhātūs keep the structure of these kingdoms intact, hels to procreate and thus allow the consciousness in these bodies to carry on their life. That is why these 7 tissues are called "limbs" - not literally but functionally!

This is fine in regard to the kingdom aspect, but how can we relate the 7 limbs to the Vāk aspect? Consider an uttered word. It can be uttered in 7 frequencies called "**notes**" or precisely "**Swarās**". A note in music is a particular gradation of pitch in our vocal sound. Once we start at a certain pitch, the other six notes' positions, in the scaling of their pitch, are fixed. After the seven notes, again the first note repeats with higher amplitude but of the same frequency. That is why Music has only 7 notes. What about the mental blueprint? For every physical entity there is a corresponding mental blueprint. If not, from where is the physical aspect taking its concrete shape? We can indeed imagine a whole song in our mind with all its various notes. Therefore Madhyamā as well as Vaikharī Vāk are composed of 7 notes. That means, the Vāk also has 7 limbs without which it can not be thought of or uttered forth.

This is what is to be meditated upon when MU says that Vaiśvānara has 7 limbs.

It has 19 mouths or doors

Doors exist to houses or objects. What does it mean to say Vaiśvānara, the fire of life, has 19 doors? Again we need to understand in an esoteric sense. In the original Sanskrit aphorism, the word **Mukha** is used. Mukha does not only mean face or mouth but also a door-way in the sense that it is an outer representative of that which is inside. Our house door acts as the first representative of the whole house as well as the dwellers of the house. That is why we give "door-address", don't we, when people need to reach us? Similarly, the 19 doors imply the 19 representatives of some hidden aspects. Now the question is what are these hidden aspects and what are these 19 doors?

Ancient seers encode multiple things in one utterance. That is an art missing from the present era. If we look closely, 19 = 10 + 9. Because we are speaking of wide awake state (Jāgṛt), let us focus on human kingdom and Vaikharī Vāk, because the animal kingdom and Madhyamā Vāk are subsets of the former anyway (Jāgṛt-lower)! In humans, the numbers 9 and 10 correspond to the primary orifices they have on the physical body which act as doorways to the inner functionalities. In both males and females, the 9 doors are common, they are: 2 eye-slots, 2 nostril slots, 2 ear slots, 1 mouth slot, 2 excretory slots. But in Females there is an extra slot for the birth of humans. This is the 10th secret doorway. Therefore in saying 19 doors, the seers imply the 9 common doors and the 10th special door in humans (and animals of course). These slots are doorways because they either input information in terms of light, sound, food, etc., or output stuff such as excreta or humans. That is why they act as Mukhās to the corresponding functionalities.

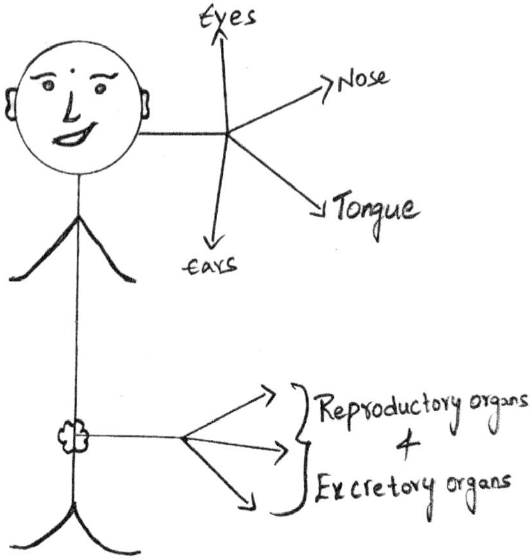

The secret that Vaiśvānara is in essence the Unit existence is also embodied in saying that he has 19 doors i.e., **19 = 1 + 9 = 10 = 1 + 0 = 1**. The One (1) in all is born again and again as the multiple beings which we have called Vaiśvānara. This cyclical repetition is symbolised by circular Zero (0). Therefore, Lord Omnipresent is 1 whereas Vaiśvānara in his full gross manifestation and wide awoken consciousness is 10 (hence 10 is often called complete number). This story of complete creation is called **Daśāṃguḷa Nyāyaṃ** - *the law of TEN inches*, in the Vēda (for example in purusha sukta we see "***....Atyatiṣṭaḥ Daśāṃguḷaṃ***").

Finally MU is saying that this Vaiśvānara is enjoying the worldly objects. Enjoyment means to identify with the object of contact. But how can Vaiśvānara enjoy with just 7 dhatūs and 9 or 10 orifices? We have overlooked something! That is why to jolt us into the right path of thinking MU puts forth this point in the aphorism that the fire of life is enjoying the worldly pleasures through the 19 doors and 7 limbs! That means, the 19 doors and 7 limbs we discussed are only the structural foundations of Vaiśvānara but do not help him to enjoy the world or identify with the worldly objects. So what is the missing set from our exploration? Let us find out.

The 7 limbs for enjoyment are: the 5 elements corresponding to Earth, Water, Fire, Air and Space; 1 cosmic mind and 1 universal Self. These 7 limbs are actually properties of the created universe without which the universe ceases to exist. But Vaiśvānara being an epitome of manifested creation, he imbibes these principles in him as the receiving pole. For example, air has a giving pole which is utilised by humans as respiration. So humans are at the receiving pole. If air does not have the property to give itself to the pressure difference, no human lung or diaphragms is capable enough to suk in the air. Similarly the same is true with respect to any other principle we imbibe from creation. So, the 7 limbs of Vaiśvānara to enjoy the world are the 7 receiving poles corresponding to the 7 giving poles of the creation. Only when this polarity is matched can we enjoy the magnetism present in the art of cherishing the creation around us. This is what is secretly taught to us in MU.

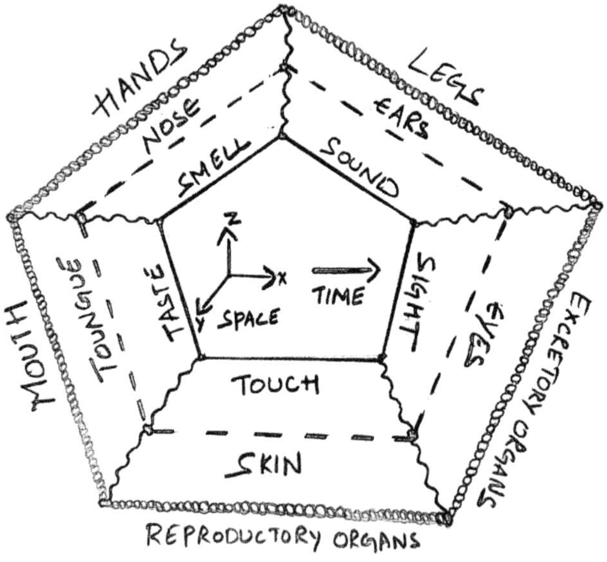

In similar line of thought, the 19 doors of enjoyment are nothing but

1. 5 dynamic organs - hands, legs, 2 excretory and 1 reproductive

2. 5 sensual organs - eyes, nose, ear, tongue and skin
3. 5 senses themselves - sight, smell, audibility, taste and touch
4. Sense of 3-spatial directions - length-breadth-height
5. Sense of Time (though it has 3 parts as pointed n first aphorism, it is experienced only at the moment and hence is considered as 1 i.e., like an arrow of time moving in one direction)

One may wonder as to how sense of direction and time is a doorway to enjoyment. If not for these senses, there is no joy at all. For example, consider the case where there is no sense of time or direction to us. Could we grow or move or contemplate the immediate past or future thought? No. What is the difference between us and a rock then? Therefore they also act as doorways to our enjoyment.

Thus, the different sets of entities are put together in one single aphorism and we need to carefully extract the information by a synthetic intuition rather than analysis.

In summary, it seems that Vaiśvānara is the fullest form of gross creation, acting as fire of life, is embodied in 19 doors and has 7 limbs and he is always in the mode of enjoying the worldly pleasures!

∞∞∞

4. The Inner Brilliance - Taijasa

Svapnasthānōntaḥ Prajñaḥ Saptāṃga Ēkōnaviṃśatimukhaḥ Praviviktabhuk Taijaso Dvītīyaḥ Pādah

Word to Word Meaning:

Svapnasthānaḥ = *the realm of existence which is dreamy;* **Antaḥprajñaḥ** = *the in-ward turned awareness;* **Saptāṃga** = *7 limbs;* **Ēōnaviṃśati** = *19;* **Mukhaḥ** = *mouths (or doors);* **Praviviktabhuk** = *enjoys solitude (or subtle objects);* **Taijasaḥ** = *the glowing one;* **Dvitīyaḥ** = *second;* **Pādaḥ** = *part.*

Import:

The second part is called Taijasa, the glowing one. Its realm of existence is a dreamy state. Its state of awareness is inward. It also has 7 limbs and 19 mouths (or doors). It enjoys solitude (or subtle objects).

Explanation:

The second of the 4-folds of the self or 4-ways of descent of the Universal self into the individualised self is now being described. It seems that this second pāda is characterised by the following characteristics.

The second fold of self is all brilliant - "Taijasa"

While we understood that the last one-fourth of the descent of creation or the grossest manifestation of the Universe (i.e., Vaiśvānara) as the "fire of life", we need to now understand that the stage preceding it is the "**Flame of Life**". Flame is Taijasa i.e., glowing in nature. What is the difference between fire and flame? Fire is physical material's state of existence whereas flame is the radiation of heat and light emanating from it. When you look at a person, his body is the fire of existence. But, the personality of the person you know is not the body but the behavioral pattern expressed through the body. This subtle pattern is what you remember when you relate your association with a person. This is nothing but the radiation of his personality emanating from his body. This is the flame of life we are speaking here. It seems that the stage that precedes the grossest manifestation is subtle in nature, because it is more radiant and brilliant.

The consciousness of this mode of self is always in a DREAMY state

The Svapna state or dreamy state, as we have seen earlier, is associated with Plant kingdom and Paśyantī Vāk. The state of consciousness is said to be dreamy for the plant kingdom. That means, there is a lower degree of localisation to its awareness. Vaiśvānara is fully awake and hence can experience the concept of locality or position. But the Taijasa is dreamy and hence it is hard to concretize the experience into a particular time or place. The same is true in terms of Vāk i.e., in the stage of Paśyaṃtī Vāk the idea or subject of utterance is not concrete and it is hazy. But is radiant in the sense, it can think of anything due to freedom of thought. Before the formation of a mental blueprint, the Vāk has its freedom to choose any idea/topic, though finally it fixes on one particular idea due to other factors such as necessity or the need of situation or inner desires. In that sense, it is Taijasa - unrestricted. Brilliance is the nature of unrestricted-ness. Light when restricted by dust or a cloth is less brilliant. But when free to radiate it is more brilliant. In that sense, the Paśyaṃtī Vāk is also Taijasa in its nature.

Its gaze is inward

The gaze of Vaiśvānara was said to be outward. This is to suggest that its stage of consciousness can comprehend the localization and pinpointing (in outer-space or time) property. But Taijasa's gaze is inward, meaning it can not quantify the experiences and hence exists inside the body's frame. Here body includes all the 7 dhātūs. What exists inside the body's frame? MIND exists. But when we spoke about Vaiśvānara's limbs and all, we have already assumed the mind's association right? Otherwise how could it enjoy the worldly pleasures? So the mind that is being spoken here is the **inner-mind** or the **subtler mind**. This is the mind that starts to work your progress when you meditate. Instead of calling it outer or inner mind it is more meaningful to call the **negative and positive poles of the one mind respectively**. The negative pole is directed outward whereas the positive pole is directed inward. This polarity of the mind is nothing but the steering wheel of consciousness. Mind steers consciousness into different planes of experiences. Depending on the gaze of the mind, the consciousness resides in a particular plane of existence. In terms of Vāk, the Paśyaṃtī Vāk is inward because it is not yet born out of the mind. Mental blueprint and physical utterance are born out of this inner gaze.

It has 7 limbs and 19 doors and It enjoys solitude (subtle objects).

Previously we have discussed the 7 limbs and 19 doors associated with Vaiśvānara in the light of Vāk or kingdoms. Let us discuss the same in relation to the Taijasic state.

The clue given is that the Taijasic state enjoys solitude. What does solitude imply? Take three different sweets: Sugar, Gulabjamun and Jalebi. Vaiśvānara experiences these as three different objects whereas Taijasa experiences these as three different gradations of one quality called "sweetness". So the common thread it enjoys is the sweet-quality. This is independent of the number of varieties that exist in the gross world. This is what is meant by Taijasa enjoying solitude or loneliness - i.e., the "number" aspect has no influence in its experience.

Therefore enjoying solitude is understood as equivalent to enjoying subtle objects. What is a subtle object? When you taste sugar in our previous example, the negative pole of the mind corresponding to the tongue of Vaiśvānara state touches sugar while the positive pole of the mind corresponding to the Taijasa state enjoys the "sweetness" of sugar. Where does the sweetness exist? In sugar? No, in our positive pole of the mind or the inner mind. Can you quantify the inner minds' experience? You may quantify as to how many sugar crystals the physical tongue has touched but not the amount of sweetness (only its relative degree). The qualitative terms such as sweeter or less sweet, etc., are hazy (dreamy) in their descriptions! This is what is meant by subtle objects - a principle behind a physical counterpart and this indicates enjoyment of solitude.

The 7 limbs it has are the principles to create the 7 limbs of Vaiśvānara. Only when there is a magnetic principle in a substance can it act as a magnet. Similarly only when there is a principle or root cause emanating the corresponding principle can the principle manifest itself physically. This subtle set of 7 principles which generate the 7 dhātūs i.e., principle of generation of blood or principle of generation of muscles, etc., along with the principle of elements, mind and self are considered here as the limbs of Taijasic state of consciousness. Similarly the principle of seven musical notes which can be uttered in mind, even though there is nothing physically present in this mind to vibrate in a particular frequency which would then generate the particular note, are the 7 limbs of Taijasic state of Paśyaṃtī Vāk.

In similar lines of correlation, the 19 doors of Taijasa state can be understood as the subtle counterparts of the previously described 19 doors of Vaiśvānara. The 10+9 orifices have specific functions. Each functionality occurs because of the principle of function. For example, eyeslots exist for eyes to see. The principle of unified vision through the sight of the two eyes is the functionality behind the eye slots. This is the door for the Taijasic state in terms of eye slots. The same goes with all other door ways that we have discussed previously. In that case, how are there 10+9 functionalities of Taijasa? A keen student of truth should observe this explanation and ask me "If the principle of unified vision through two eyes is the door for Tijasa, are there two doors or one door ?

If two doors exist, then 10+9 subtle doors tallies with that of 10+9 gross doors of Vaiśvānara. But if the principle of sight is 1 and similarly, hearing etc., are considered, don't we fall short of a few doors to the calculation of 19 subtle doors?".

The answer can be given by considering the Tantric tenets belonging to the wisdom of Goddess - Śrī Vidyā. For example, consider the 22nd name of Lalitā Sahasranāma (1000 esoteric names of the World Mother), which says "***Tāṭaṃka Yugaḷībhūta Tapanōḍupa Maṇḍalā***". It indicates that the world mother has SUN and MOON as her ear rings attached to each of her ears. What does it signify? That the two ears behave and perceive different subtle signals. Right ear on which SUN is attached, is sensitive to the solar principle whereas the left ear on which the Moon is attached, is sensitive to the lunar principle. That is why when an initiation is given to a student, depending on the type of initiation, either the Mantra is chosen to be imparted through the left or the right ear. The same can be seen in the Virāṭ form of Puruṣa according to Āyurvēda or Bhagawadgīta. For example, Virāṭ (the cosmic egg) has SUN as his right eye and moon as his left eye. In Kuṇḍalinī Yōga also it is said that the left and right nostrils are governed by Iḍa and Piṃgaḷa nāḍīs (nāḍīs are subtle channels that carry the Prāṇa or the life force). What do we understand from so many scriptural clues? We conclude that each door, though represents similar functions at times, is governed by different root principles and hence there are exactly 19 (10+9) subtle doors behaving as the causes for the 19 physical doors.

So MU is suggesting that when we meditate via the 19 gross doors and 7 gross limbs, we should also meditate on the root principles behind their origin so that their true nature is properly understood by us which we then can utilize to speed the spiritual evolution.

∞∞∞

5. The Conscious Intelligence - Prajña

Yatra Suptō Na Kañcana Kāmaṃ Kāmayatē Na Kañcana Svapnaṃ Paśyati Tatsuṣuptaṃ Suṣuptasthāna Ēkībhūtaḥ Prajñānaghana Ēvānandamayō Hyānandabhuk Cētōmukhaḥ Prājñastṛtīyaḥ Pādaḥ

Word To Word Meaning:

Yatra = *where;* Suptaḥ = *sleeping one;* Kaṃcana = *any;* Na+Kāmaṃ = *no desire;* Kāmayatē = *desired;* Kañcana = *any;* Na+Svapnaṃ = *no dream;* Paśyati = *seen;* Tat = *that;* Suṣuptaṃ = *is the state of Suṣupti;* Suṣuptasthānaḥ = *the realm of existence is deep-sleep;* Ēkībhūtaḥ = *unified;* Prajñānaghanaḥ = *the condensed awareness;* Ēva = *indeed;* Ānandamayaḥ = *the form is bliss;* Hi+Ānandabhuk = *verily the enjoyer of the bliss;* Cētaḥ = *consciousness;* Mukhaḥ = *mouth (or door);* Prajñaḥ = *the state of Prajṇa (conscious-intelligence);*

Tṛtīyaḥ = *third;* **Pādaḥ** = *part.*

Import:

Suṣupti is a sleeping state where there is no desire desired nor any dream dreamt (seen). That Suṣupti exists in the realm of a deep-sleep state having a unified form of condensed awareness (being strongly aware of oneness). Indeed it is verily the bliss as well as the object of its joy is also the bliss. This is the conscious-intelligence which is the third part having consciousness as its doorway.

Explanation:

The third of the 4-folds of the self or 4-ways of descent of the Universal self into the individualised self is now being described.

The third fold of self is PRAJÑA

What is Prajña? **Jña** means to know. **Pra** is used as a decorative add-on to implicate "specially". So **Prajña** means to know something specially. What does "specially" mean? It means to know something in the light of consciousness. Therefore, Prajña can be termed as "**conscious-intelligence**" i.e., the third part corresponding to the unfoldment of the self is conscious intelligence.This is that state of the Ātma which is the first differentiation from the Universal self. If you imagine an ocean and a set of ripples, Prajña forms the first cause of ripples in the ocean of existence. All the aforementioned states are but different gradations of this Prajña.

PRAJÑA is characterized by a state called "SUṢUPTI" and it is a deep-sleep state having no dreams or desires

Therefore, Prajña corresponds to the deep-sleep or Suṣupti state of mineral kingdom and the impulse originating Parā Vāk state of the utterance of creation. Consciousness in the mineral kingdom is in a deep slumber state. Generally it is called Jaḍa Caitanya meaning slumbering consciousness.

Here there are two aspects to be carefully understood. On one side we are saying that Prajña means a conscious-intelligence. On the other side we relate it to the mineral kingdom which are not at all intelligent and in fact are in a dull state of inertia. How to correlate these seemingly opposite concepts? This is where the purāṇās come to our rescue in the form of symbolism. Consider the concept of **Arthnārīśvarā** - The lord hermaphrodite (represented by the Yin (dark) & Yang (bright)). When the creation occurs as a ripple in the Brahman, it does so by separating itself into two polarities. This is symbolised as the triple aspect of Bhrahman, Śiva and Śakti. Bhraman will be discussed later. Śiva is depicted in the purāṇās as someone who favours crematory grounds and hence is symbolic to the Jaḍa or slumbering consciousness. But Śakti is the life of Śiva as pointed by Śankarācārya. Therefore she represents the bright intelligence which acts through the Jaḍa to maintain its state of slumber as well as to awaken it into other kingdoms through the course of evolution (mineral to plant to animal to human to GOD). Look at crystals or diamonds or beach sand, etc. There is a beauty in all these - beauty of form, beauty of texture, beauty of color, etc. This beauty of creation behind the veil of Jaḍa or slumbering consciousness is the light of consciousness which is "**intelligent**". But without the inactive sand there is no beauty called smooth beach-sand or colorful coral beach. That means Śiva and Śakti cannot be separated and one without the other is meaningless. Thus, Prajña is symbolised by both mineral kingdom as well as the intelligence which germinates and maintains the properties of the mineral kingdom!

In terms of Vāk, Prajña relates to Parā Vāk. We saw that Parā Vāk is the first impulse that occurs in the word that was with the GOD. How did the impulse originate? It is because of the intelligence that exists behind the origin of Vāk and hence Parā is indeed intelligent. If we think that Parā is random in its intelligence, then the creation evolving from such a random impulse should also be chaotic and unstructured. But the whole universe is filled with ordered beauty! The hidden symmetry even behind seeming chaos suggests that the first impulse itself is nothing but conscious-intelligence. Therefore Parā Vāk is indeed Prajnã.

The joy and delight of existing in this mode occurs by virtue of being itself as oneness

We have seen that Vaiśvānara enjoys the physical objects whereas Taijasa enjoys the subtle objects. But what does Prajña enjoy? It seems that it enjoys the state of oneness. Oneness of what? Oneness of consciousness in seeming separateness. When we are awake, we tend to enjoy the sensual objects like air conditioners, cool drinks, snacks, etc. When we really start to enjoy any of these objects, we tend to actually enjoy their qualities such as coolness, sweetness, sourness, etc. But these objects take us only upto certain level in the depth of the real meaning of "Joy". How much of sweetness can you withstand or how much quantity of a snack can you munch on? After a limit you will start to lose the joy you first had when you were entangled with it. But beyond the physical and subtle world of objects, exists a world of unified thread which connects the seemingly separate entities as one. This is called Prajña. When the consciousness is in the state of Prajña, it has a larger amount of JOY because it is experiencing the ALL. When we all live as a united family we enjoy the bliss of unity even though there may be some minor discrepancies underneath. But because of those discrepancies if the families separate and establish themselves as the modern day nuclear families, what is the result? We all exist without love and affection of our own kith and kin and we crave for such attention all the time and eventually dislike the separated lifestyle. So, joy exists in unity of things rather than in separateness.

The question then is through what mechanism does Prajña exist in a unified state? To understand this, the clue given to us is "deep sleep". When we are half awake/dreamy we do not get the feel of satisfaction pertaining to our sleep. This is because the separate entity called "I am" is existing either in an active wakeful state or a hazy wakeful (dreamy) state. But slowly as we go to such stages of sleep which are beyond the dreams, the "I am"-ness disappears. Where did it go? It went to the domains where Parā Vāk exists i.e., the sense of "I am" is dissolved in the Prajña. Are there different Prajñas? Do you and do I have different deep-sleep states? No. Once we go beyond the dreams,the deep-sleep experience is the same because no one can speak about it while in it! So, Prajña is only one but it has the ability to associate with separate entities in order to energise them. There is only one current - called flow of electrons. But, when it enters different instruments, it behaves differently (sound, light, heat, etc.). The same is true with Prajña in us.

Though Suṣupti is associated with deep-sleep, it does not mean "sleep" in our regular terms. It means a state where the individual "I am" is ignorant of itself. The experience we have in deep-sleep pertaining to sleep is the lower side of Prajña - Śiva state or mineral kingdom state. It can be called inactive joy or slumbering joy. But when the same is experienced while active, it relates to Śakti or active joy. Let me give a neat example to put all these concepts into one frame for you to contemplate.

Imagine that you are in a nice musical concert. Initially Vaiśvānara exists as your bodily self in the concert. He looks here and there through your senses and interacts with your friends. The moment the concert starts, he becomes alert and silent. He starts to listen. When the performer is artistic, the music he produces resonates with our inner core. This lets Vaiśvānara dissolve into Taijasa who actually experiences the "music" in the song of the concert by virtue of its association with the subtle objects. In this stage, you will lose your personality i.e., the sense of "I am so and so", "I came with so and so", etc., are dissolved but you will keep hearing the music in the song. When this music is too nice, it acts to dissolve the Taijasa state into the state of Prajña. In that state, neither you nor the experience of the music exists. What exists? Music alone exists. This is what is meant by Prajña state or deep sleep in active form. How is it active? After the song stops, you will come out of the Prajña into Vaiśvānara state. Though you would not remember what was exactly played, a sense of satisfaction exists in you. Duration of the song - be it 1 hr or 2 hrs, would not be remembered, nor the specific technicalities performed. What you remember is the "FEEL" of the music. If the music has taken you only to the levels of Taijasa, you would remember all those details which means you did not become one with music. But in the former condition of Prajña, you became one with the music and hence the existence of music alone implied that you were in the music as the music itself. This is the actual depth of Suṣupti being spoken here.

The door for this is the consciousness

Previously we have seen that Vaiśvānara and Taijasa have 19 doors, the 10 + 9 schematic. But there is only ONE door for Prajña it seems. Because it is an entity that dwells in Unity, ONE must be the door indeed! What is that door? It seems it is verily the consciousness - Cētana. Prajña is conscious intelligence which expresses itself through Consciousness. Image a voltage difference between two points. When this difference is non-zero there will be a current flow. If consciousness is compared to this voltage difference, the flow of current can be compared to the Prajña. Depending on the voltage difference, the current flow is regulated. Similarly, though Prajña is ONE in essence and its door is ONE which is consciousness, depending on the other layers (Taijasa and Vaiśvānara), the degree of Prajña's awakening is dependent. This is the story of the trio - physical, subtle and consciousness!

∞∞∞

6. Prajña As The Light Of Gāyatrī

Ēṣa Sarvēśvaraḥ Ēṣa Sarvajñaḥ Ēṣōntaryāmyēṣa Yōniḥ Sarvasya Prabhavāpyayau Hi Bhūtānāṃ

Word To Word Meaning:

Ēṣaḥ = *this;* **Sarva+Īśvraḥ** = *lord of all;* **Ēṣaḥ** = *this;* **Sarvajñaḥ** = *omniscient;* **Ēṣaḥ** = *this;* **Antaryāmiḥ** = *Omnipresent (indweller of all);* **Ēṣaḥ** = *this;* **Yōniḥ** = *birth womb;* **Sarvasya** = *of all;* **Prabhavāpyayau** = *the cause and dissolution;* **Hi** = *verily;* **Bhūtānāṃ** = *of all.*

Import:

This (Prajña) is the lord of all that is. It is omniscient as well as omnipresent. It is the birth womb from which all is born and in which all dissolves.

Explanation:

As you have seen it was easy to understand the first fold and slightly difficult to understand the second fold. The third fold was little more difficult. To understand a physically uttered word is far easier than understanding the reason behind the utterance itself! Therefore to help us in our struggling path to understand the previous aphorism, a helping aphorism is given here. This should aid in unknotting the difficult knots.

The "this" in the stanza is pointed to the 3rd fold. So, aphorism-6 is like 5b.

Prajña exists in all things as the Parā Vāk stage or deep slumber (active/passive) stage. In humans it may exist as active slumber while awake and may exist as a passive slumber while asleep. In the mineral kingdom it is always passive slumber. So on and so forth in the intermediate kingdoms. In this way Prajña permeates all the kingdoms from mineral to human and pervades all the stages of the word from Parā to Vaikharī. Not only permeating or pervading, it is the cause for all the gradations of consciousness or stages of the creation as the word of god. This is the reason to summarise the following key points in this stanza

- **Prajña is the lord of all beings**
- **It is the all knowing and all wise lord**
- **It is the permeating in-dweller of all**

These are self explanatory given the previously explained details are properly understood in the light of meditative contemplation. The next point needs some explanation.

This is the birth womb of creation and dissolution of manifestations

How is Prajña the birth womb of creation? We have seen that Parā Vāk is the birth stage of Vāk as well as active/passive slumber is the birth stage of consciousness. In that sense, Prajña acts as the starting point from which the rest of the creation or the levels of consciousness unfolds themselves. A womb acts also as a nourishing agent to the would-be baby. It imparts the potential qualities of the baby in seed form. Therefore this suggests that Prajña is not only the master of all the other folds, but it is also the etcher and carpenter of the other folds. All the potential qualities of Vaiśvānara or Taijasa states exist as seed forms in Prajña. For example, say a person has a tendency to help others unconditionally even though none of his family members encouraged him to do so since childhood. From where do such traits come to him? They reside in his Prajña as seed principles which sprout when proper environmental conditions are favoured (opportunities and economic abilities, etc). These inturn depend on his Karmic cycles of course. In that sense the Prajña acts as a vault of seed principles for this creation and hence is called the birth womb of the creation!

How can a birth womb be associated with dissolution of all? Previously we have stated that there are two slumbers - active and passive. Active slumber (Śakti) is the birth womb. Passive slumber (Śiva) is the destruction of all and hence the purāṇic symbolism of cemetery residence of Śiva is apt! What does it mean to be a bank of dissolution? It means that Prajña again acts as the crematory ground for all the manifested principles to dissolve and retake the shape of seed principles. To understand this, meditate on your sleep-cycle. When awake we are active. Prajña's energy is diversified into our mundane activity. When we sleep the self dissolves and so also its many principles - what we call our nature. In deep sleep, which is true sleep, no principle exists on its own i.e., the many icebergs of the quantitative and qualitative world dissolve into the ocean of consciousness. But remember they are not destroyed but only dissolved. If our qualities were destroyed, could we wake as the same personality after the duration of deep-sleep? No! Then, during the period of deep-sleep where did these seed principles go? They were engulfed into the womb of the Prajña, only to take birth again in the next wake! This is what is meant by Prajña is also the bed of dissolution. It is akin to the path of the sun as observed from the Earth and its relation to our consciousness! The sunrise is the wake and the sunset is the sleep. When we meditate on this aspect of Prajña, it is better to relate to SUN's position. So in the morning meditation (sunrise), we should meditate on our waking aspect and in the evening meditation (sunset) we should meditate on how we dissolve back into our Prajña.

The sunrise and sunset timings are called Sandhyā or the twilight. These are very important phases of the day for a spiritualist. The age-old worshipping of the inner-self via the glory of the inner-SUN is encoded in the famous Gāytrī mantra which is often advised to be uttered during these twilight hours. When you relate AUM to the concept of inner-Sun and Gāyatrī you will see that the meditation of Prajña's dual role, as suggested by MU, is equivalent to the essence of this twilight hour worship. So, the present aphorism is something like a secret initiation into the light of Gāyatrī.

∞∞∞

7. The core philosophy of Non-Dualism - Advaita

Nāntaḥ Prajñaṃ Na Bahiṣprajñaṃ Nobhayataḥprajñaṃ Na Prajñānaghanaṃ Na Prajñaṃ Nā-prajñaṃ Adṛṣṭaṃ Avyavahārayaṃ Agrāhyaṃ Alakṣaṇaṃ Acintyaṃ Avyapadeśyaṃ Ēkātmapratyayasāraṃ Prapañcopaśamaṃ Śāntaṃ Śivaṃ Advaitaṃ Caturthaṃ Manyantē Sa Ātmā Sa Vijñeyaḥ

Word To Word Meaning:

Na+Antaḥ+Prajñaṃ = *awareness that is not inward;* Na+Bahiṣ+Prajñaṃ = *awareness that is not outward;* Na+Ubhayataḥ+Prajñaṃ = *awareness that is neither (inward nor outward);* Na+Prajñanāghanam = *not the condensed awareness;* Na+Prajñaṃ = *neither the conscious-intelligence;* **Na+A+Prajñaṃ** = *nor the unconscious intelligence;* **A+Dṛṣṭaṃ** = *not seen;* **A+Vyavahāryaṃ** = *cannot be spoken of;* **A+Grāhyaṃ** = *cannot be comprehended;* **A+Lakṣaṇaṃ** = *does not has any quality;* **A+Cintyaṃ** = *cannot be thought of;* **Avyapadēśyaṃ** = *cannot be described of (has no name);* **Ēkātma + Pratyaya + Sāraṃ** = *the essence of the unity of the ONE grand soul;* **Pra+Pañca+Upaśamaṃ** = *in which the world of five grand elements (i.e., creation) dissolves;* **Śāntaṃ** = *peaceful;* **Śivaṃ** = *auspicious;* **A+Dvaitaṃ** = *being non-dual;* **Caturthaṃ** = *fourth part;* **Manyantē** = *is considered to be;* **Saḥ** = *He;* **Ātmā** = *the soul;* **Saḥ** = *he;* **Vijñēyaḥ** = *the true object of exploration.*

Import:

The fourth part is considered (by the seers) to be verily the soul and the true object of exploration of all (aspirants). It is awareness that is neither turned inward nor outward nor neither. It is not the condensed awareness. It is not the conscious-intelligence nor its opposite. It can not be seen nor can anything be spoken about it (in concrete sense) because it is incomprehensible. It has no qualities. It can not be either thought of or described about. It is the essence of unity of the ONE grand soul. In it the whole creation dissolves. It is peaceful and auspicious. There is no dual to it (as it is ONE).

Explanation:

Now comes the fourth part and final fold of the self. There is a very peculiar trait in the Vēda i.e., whenever the concept of the absolute abstract inexpressible GOD needs to be spoken of, it is spoken in the tone of negative and double-negative statements. The same was followed later on in the purāṇās or itihāsās. For example, in the Mahābhārata the twin gods Aśvins are named Nāsatyās. Nāsatya = Na + Asatya = Na + A + Satya. The "Na" and "A" are two negations. It is something like when I say "I do not not like to run", it would mean "I neither like nor dislike to run" - so shows a neutral ground. Similarly, Na + A + Satya means that which is neither true nor false and therefore Aśvins are the Gods who are beyond the sense of truthhood of our world.

In the present aphorism, there are many negatives and double negatives. Let us go through one by one and then come back to the common exploration.

- **This is Prajña that which is neither inward nor outward nor both**
- **This is Prajña that which is neither a condensed state of something nor itself nor not itself**
- **It cannot be perceived, it can not be spoken about, it can not be caught and it does not have any qualities**
- **It can not be thought of and it has no name.**
- **It is the essence of the unity of the ONE self**
- **It is the background in which the world of five qualities dissolve**
- **It is calm, auspicious and non-dual (there is no "other" than this)**

- **It is the fourth fold which is the true self and the true object of all of our exploration.**

Until now we have explored four folds of the self and the four stages of creation which we could, to some degree or the other, comprehend. Also we have seen that there was an increase in the degree of difficulty in comprehending the subtler stages or folds. The highest difficulty we faced was for the Parā Vāk or the Prajña stage. It seemed almost that the Prajña stage was equivalent to that of lord absolute. But is it so? We have seen in the form of conscious-intelligence it needs the created beings and their dynamism to exist i.e., Śiva and Śakti aspects needed to exist in order for Prajña to work out its characteristics. Similarly, in the form of Parā Vāk, Prajña needed a medium in which the impulse had to originate as the primary cause of the first ripple in the ocean of creation. Therefore, in both the cases, there is a dual-aspect: **the background** and **the dynamic element** (active/passive) of Prajña. But lord absolute should have the aforementioned negatives and double-negatives. None of these suit Prajña stage. For example, the absolute is said to be non-dual. But we have seen that Prajña depends on the dual characteristics of creation and hence can not be non-dual.

Therefore there is something beyond this Prajña which is causing it to acquire its characteristics. It seems that this something or someone has no name, no form, no shape, no quality, no state, no thought, etc., and at the same time that something or someone is all these as well as neither these!! How wonderfully put by the seers! Let us see how to decode the mystery in this. In the state of Prajña, we have seen an example of Musical concert. Take the same example again. When you entered the stage of Suṣupti, the stage where you became the music, you had a wonderful feeling afterwards, even though you could not remember the specifics of the musical piece. But when this Suṣupti is touched by the state of Brahman (by his grace through the musical piece) then one enters the stage of **Turīya or the kingdom of God**! What is the experience? Consider the aforementioned negatives and double-negatives. That would be the description of such a state. Instead of the trio of you, music and surroundings existing (Vaiśvānara), instead of you and music alone existing (Taijasa), instead of music alone existing i.e., you become the music (Prajña) there will be BRAHMAN alone. In him everything is dissolved. No music, no you, no surrounding but the absolute GOD alone exists and pervades.

Consider a colorful garment. When you start to analyse it, you will see that the garment is actually a set of woven threads and color is just a coating. The threads are but processed cotton fiber. The cotton is nothing but a set of molecules which themselves are made of a set of atoms. Atoms are but a set of subatomic particles which are nothing but modes of energy. Therefore the whole garment is but a mode of ENERGY. What is energy? It is the Prajña of BRAHMAN. You can use a garment but not the energy directly. In fact, all the energy we use is either one form of energy or the other - heat, light, electricity, magnetism, etc. but not energy in its raw form. Can we comprehend absolute energy in its pure state! No. Then how can we comprehend the source of this energy BRAHMAN? Does this mean we can never understand BRAHMAN? Then what use of speaking and what use of the MU's aphorisms or yōga or tantra? BRAHAMAN cannot be understood or known or contemplated upon, but we can **become** BRAHMAN! This is the key point to remember by us in our meditative approach. There is a story in the Bhagavata Purāṇa pertaining to this specific keynote of BRAHMAN. It runs as follows.

Once, sage Nārada, in his previous life, sits to perform a penance in the search of Brahman. He slowly transcends from the stages of physical / gross to the subtle stages of inner self. At one point he became BRAHMAN. But as his search started with a curiosity to see who this BRAHMAN is, the same thought again arose in his otherwise absolute self. Immediately he fell down to the stage of Prajña/Suṣupti and then into the stages of mind & body and thus missed the experience of Brahman. He wept and cried to regain that state and feel it. But can he feel? While asleep, can you feel the sleep? No. So, when he was BRAHMAN, how can he feel BRAHMAN? So the god (one of his forms) spoke from the sky that Nārda had to wait for the next cycle of creation in order to establish himself as BRAHMAN for a longer duration.

This story embeds the import presented above in regard to BRAHMAN. So, there is only becoming GOD and no "knowing" or "tasting" or "feeling" GOD. In such a stage, we are truth as well as the un-truth. How? Take for example Rama and Sita. We know Sita is the wife of Rama and Rama is the husband of Sita. But Rama is also a father and Sita is also a mother to Lava and Kusha. Rama is also a son to Dasaratha and Sita is also a daughter to Janaka. In their essence, both are but BRAHMAN. But for us neither Rama nor Sita is a son or a daughter or a brother, etc. The relations that we have pointed to are relative in nature. Rama is the husband of Sita and not to anyone else. So, the truth that he is a husband and again the truth that he is not a husband, both exist to Rama as a person who is living in this dual world (Brahman after creation). But Rama is neither is the absolute truth belonging to the non-dual Brahman (Brahman before creation)! This is the most enigmatic nature of the abstract concept of BRAHMAN.

This Brahman or the final fold or the only existing entity is the true Ātma and the true object of exploration. It means that the goal of the wide awoken consciousness - we humans - is to trace its evolutionary stages and dissolve into the absolute BRAHMAN. It is not for the sake of mere information that the stages are given here but for us to put into practice. Irrespective of our attempt, we do tend in this direction of realization because, we are ever in search of happiness and pure happiness implies a stage of no-duality. But when we learn from the masters and seers and practice their tenets, we speed up the process with much less struggle. So, no seer forces you to practice, but if you go to them with a zeal to practice, they would definitely guide you. MU is one such guiding lights for sincere aspirants!

∞∞∞

8. The Threefold Division Of Om: A-U-M

Sōyamātmādhyakṣaramōṃkārōd-himātraṃ Pādā Mātrā Mātrāśca Pādā Akāra Ukāra Makāra Iti

Word To Word Meaning:

Saḥ = *he;* **Ayaṃ** = *this;* **Ātmā** = *soul;* **Adhyakṣaraṃ** = *relating to syllables;* **Ōṃkāraḥ** = *AUM;* **Adhimātraṃ** = *relating to the duration of utterance (Mātrā);* **Pādā** = *the parts;* **Mātrā** = *the measures of syllables;* **Mātrāśca** = *And the measures of the syllables;* **Pādā** = *are the parts;* **Akāra** = *A;* **Ukāra** = *U;* **Makāra** = *M.*

Import:

He, the eternal soul, is verily the divine Ōṃ. It is related to the syllables and their utterances via the measures of duration. It is composed of three modes of utterance, namely, A-U-M.

Explanation:

The first aphorism spoke about AUM. But the aphorism 2 to 7 spoke about Ātma in terms of its creation (unfoldment or descent from Brahman) as well as its existence (degree of consciousness). At first sight it seems odd to have started with AUM and have not described anything abou AUM in almost 50% of the whole Upaniṣad! Now it is being said that the AUM mentioned in the first aphorism is actually linked to the four pādās that have been extensively explored. With this link we will see that all the while they were describing AUM itself! If not for the first aphorism, we would think that the Upanṣad is about something else. But to fix our backdrop of contemplation on AUM, it was made the object of the first stanza and later on to train us into the right attitude of approaching the true self, starting from the physical, and help us transcend to the abstract oneness, the rest of the aphorisms were given. So, the object of- as well as the means of -proper meditation have been given up to now. From hereon, the missing links will be given which would bring shape, structure and meaning to our already thorough exploration. After these links, one will be able to correlate the whole Universe, including one's self, to the most sacred AUM and thus be able to dwell in the most pious state of divine ecstasy.

The following are the linking key points mentioned in this aphorism

Whatever we said about the indestructible Ātma, which is equivalent to he/that/it,etc. (i.e., Brahman), is verily the Ōṃ which protects by the way of its measures.

The terms such as **Akṣaraṃ**, **Mātrā** have usual meanings of **syllable** and **sounds** respectively. With these manings, the first line of the aphorism would mean that the Ātma, which is equivalent to Brahman as discussed before, is verily the sound and syllable symbolised by AUM. Then, one may fall into utter confusion as to how sound or a syllable, which actually exists only to the physical/subtle world be associated with Brhman who includes and yet is beyond them? That is why no Vēdic scripture should be literally "translated" and studied but should be intuitively studied by looking in between the translated lines. Looking in between means to utilize Sanskrit's ability to encode multiple meanings to the same wordings!

Akṣara = A + Kṣara = indestructible and **Mātrā = Mā + Tra = that which protects (tra) by the way of measures (Mā)**. It seems that Brahman or the four fold self Ātma is the Akṣara and Mātrā of AUM. To understand this, we need to understand AUM in terms of these root meanings. AUM as akṣara meaning indestructible and eternal was already dealt in the first aphorism. Let us see what Matra of AUM means in its root sense. There is **measure** everywhere in this Universe.

Be it our breath, beat of heart, colors of flowers or their petal patterns, sounds of birds, periodicities of planets, Sun's yearly cycles, galactic or nebulae formations, etc. Everything is filled by measurements. We are protected by these measures means that our life depends on these measures and if there is a change in these measures, our life would turn upside down. For example, if all flowers were green (measure of frequency of light reflected by them) or if our sense of hearing were beyond 20 kilohertz, our life would not be the same-normal that we have now. Even if the Earth were a few kilometers close to the SUN, life would have evolved differently on the Earth or it would not have evolved at all! Therefore, the measurements bring structure to our life and without them, it is impossible to live. This is what is meant by MĀTRĀ. A duration of utterance of a syllable is thus also called Mātra because duration is also a measure. Just like syllables, being indestructible, are also named Akṣara, their duration of utterance are also named Mātrā. Therefore the latter are only derived meanings but not root meanings. This is very important to probe the complex labyrinth of the Vēdic mind.

In fact AUM does not occur in any of the 50 Akṣarās that Sanskrit has. Anything other than an Akṣara or a syllable is formed by two or more syllables and hence is a WORD rather than a syllable. Therefore AUM is not a syllable in actuality. Then, how can

AUM be called an Akṣara at all in the first place? This is the direct hint that the AUM, which the seer of the MU is speaking, is not the vocal sound uttered as Ōṃ i.e., a combination of the elongated syllables "Ō and Ṃ" (usually we pronounce it as ...Oooooommm-mmm...), but something that runs as its undercurrent. But having said that it is a syllable, it means that the starting step in understanding the ultimate Ōṃ is only via a vocal utterance and no other way! A mere intellectual contemplation can not help. But when the intellectual contemplation is mixed with vocal utterance of Ōṃ, it helps us open the doors to the domains imperceptible. This is the key of the Vēdic lore since the dawn of time. All the Vēdās are uttered, taught and learnt vocally. But the very content the Vēda speaks is beyond the physical realms (of sound), though includes it as a part of the whole wisdom. Just like the energy we get from food is beyond the food but the physical food is very necessary to extract that non-physical energy, so also the ŌṂ we utter in a meditative state takes us from Vaiṣvānara to Brahman and hence it protects us from the world of duality which is the cause of all the problems. A problem exists only when there are two things. What problem exists if there is only ONE? The problem itself is the solution! **This is what is meant by saying that AUM is Mātrā and AUM is Akṣaraṃ and AUM is verily Brahman.**

AUM

How to link up this Ōṃ to the previously defined stages? How to transcend from Vaiśvānara to Brahman in real life? The first step is of course to utter and meditate AUM. But what do you contemplate during meditation? It is easy to say that we are Brahman, but as you have seen in the story of Nārada that it is hard to enter into such a stage. So, Brahman can not be an object of meditation even though Brahman is the "true object" of meditation by default! To make the processes simpler, seers have asked us to follow the tenets of this MU which says that while uttering the Ōṃ aloud and listening to it, try to resonate to the idea that it is made up of three parts, i.e.,

This OM has three syllables (modes of utterance)

- *"A" - uttered as in "LUCK"*
- *"U" - uttered as in "PUT"*
- *"M" - uttered as in "MUM"*

So, it seem that ŌṂ is made up of three root syllables or modes of utterances, namely A, U and M. The forthcoming aphorisms will proceed to strengthen the hidden links.

∞∞∞

9. Syllable A - Vaiśvānara

Jāgaritasthānō Vaiśvānarōkāraḥ Prathamāmātrāptērādimattvād-vāpnōti Ha Vai Sarvānkāmānādiśca Bhavati Ya Evaṃ Vēda.

Word To Word Meaning:

Jāgaritasthānaḥ = *the realm of wakefulness;* **Vaiśvā-naraḥ** = *the being in all;* **Akāraḥ** = *is A;* **Prathamā +Mātrā** = *the first mode of utterance;* **Āptēḥ** = *due to per-vasiveness;* **Ādimattvāt** = *being the foremost (mode);* **Vā** = *who;* **Āpnōti** = *fulfill;* **Ha Vai** = *certainly;* **Sarvān +Kāmānādi** = *all desires and the like;* **Ca** = *and;* **Bhavati** = *happens;* **Yaḥ** = *who;* **Ēvaṃ** = *thus;* **Vēda** = *knows.*

Import:

The first mode of utterance "A" is verily the Vaiśvānara belonging to the realm of wakefulness due to the quality of the pervasiveness. It is the foremost mode of utterance (with respect to our direct comprehension). Who knows this concept will fulfill all the desires and the like and this happening is certain.

Explanation:

The key points of this stanza can be summarised as follows

- **The first mode of utterance "A" is verily the Vaiśvānara.**
- **He (A) is the wakeful consciousness and is all-pervasive.**
- **Those who know him will fulfill all desires.**

There is a subtle difference between the state of Vaiśvānara and the Vaiśvānara that is spoken here which is associated with "A". The previous Vaiśvānara is the mere state of creation but the present Vaiśvānara is the human who, by process of meditation, achieved oneness with it in all its glory.

Remember that the goal of an Upaniṣad is not only to give a set of useful information but also to instruct us in the art of using them practically in our life, which would then lead us to the TRUTH of the divine wisdom (Vēda). That is why it is called **Upa +ni+ṣad = that which takes you nearer (to the Vēda)**. The goal of MU is to teach us the way of meditation pertaining to the utterance of AUM and hearing it. Previously, Vaiśvānara was suggested to be a unified form of physical and mental aspects of creation. But how often do we remember that we, the humans, are

Vaiśvānara also? We often identify ourselves with the objects of senses and entangled mental emotions. To first pull us out of these wrong entanglements which are the main cause of all the misery, the first part of MU tries to make our mind busy with the categorization of the divine law of creation into the 4 pādās. This gave our mind the necessary backdrop in regard to the map of the creation. Now to use the map, a set of corresponding laws are being given.

Before meditation, we exist as a superposition of all the four pādās mentioned before. When we are in a movie, we exist in the mental stages (Madhyamā) while when we read rigorously, we exist beyond the mental stages (paśyaṃtī). Sometimes when we fight or play we exist physically (Vaikharī). Rarely in sleep we enter Parā. And often because we simultaneously multitask, we exist in a superposed state of all these modes of existence. But the desired end goal is to exist as the one thread that runs through all of these states of existence i.e., the kingdom of GOD! The only way to enter such a kingdom is to first regularise our state of being and then transform it step by step. So, before meditation, we are a haphazard set of iron filings and what meditation does is orient us in line with the divine magnetic lines of force!

When we start the meditation of AUM, the first modification that occurs in us is that we will consciously acquire the positive nature of Vaiśvānara that we have explored earlier. It seems that this is the quality of "all pervasiveness". Pervasiveness is the quality that can exist only when space and time exists. Space and time exist physically and mentally. Therefore the space-time matrix of the creation exists only to Vaiśvānara and not to any other three pādās described before. That means, the ultimate glory of Vaiśvānara exists in becoming verily the space-time rather than being associated with the elements (individual vāk or individual states of consciousness) created as the product of space-time. This happens when he "pervades". But this is the idea that we need to take as the guiding point in our meditation. Technically speaking, Vaiśvānara is already pervaded - an ocean is pervaded by water! But, the onus to experience this falls on us and that is what is meant by saying that Vaiśvānara's glory is all-pervasiveness which is what is the glory we will achieve as humans when we start to meditate the "A"-sound of AUM and awaken ourselves into the wakeful consciousness of all-pervasive Vaiśvānara!

When we slowly start to expand our consciousness by assimilating the seemingly different individual consciousness, we tend to burn away the bank of desires in us. For example, as long as food is separate from us, we feel hungry, the moment it is assimilated into us, we are satiated. But we again feel hunger when the assimilated food is converted to energy and extinguished. In the all-pervading aspect, slowly our self becomes the other beings' self and there is no question of extinguishing. Thus, such an assimilation brings in a reduction of desires. When all-pervasive nature is completely bloomed, we are verily the space-time and hence there are no desires that sprout out of us. This is what is mentioned as "**those who know this first syllable A can fulfill all the desires**".

∞∞∞

10. Syllable U - Taijasa

Svapnasthānastaijasa Ukāro Dvitīyā Mātrotkarṣādubhayatvādvotkarṣati Ha Vai Jñānasaṃtatiṃ Samānaśca Bhavati Nāsyābrahmavit Kule Bhavati Ya Ēvaṃ Vēda.

Word To Word Meaning:

Svapnasthānaḥ = *the realm of dreamy state;* **Taijasa** = *the glowing one;* **Ukāraḥ** = *is U;* **Dvitīyā+Mātraḥ** = *the second mode of utterance;* **Utkarṣad** = *superior (with respect to the previous mode);* **Ubhayavāt** = *as a fulcrum between the two;* **Vā** = *who;* **Utkarṣati** = *rises;* **Ha Vai** = *certainly;* **Jñāna+Santatiṃ** = *the descendents of those who know;* **Sa+Māna** = *the true measure ;* **Ca** = *and;* **Bhavati** = *happens;* **Asya** = *his;* **A+Brahmavit** = *those who do not know Brahman;* **Kulē** = *in the lineage of;* **Na+Bhavati** = *are not born;* **Yaḥ** = *who;* **Ēvaṃ** = *thus;* **Vēda** = *knows.*

Import:

The second mode of utterance U is the glowing one belonging to the realm of dreamy state. It is superior to the previous one and acts as a fulcrum between A and M. Certainly by knowing this U, one can rise themselves to a stage where none in their lineage are born without the knowledge of BRAHMAN.

Explanation:

The following are the key points pertaining to the second mode of utterance - "U".

- **"U" is verily Taijasa and superior to the previous one.**
- **He (U) is in a dreamy or hazy state of consciousness.**
- **This forms a fulcrum between A and M.**
- **No one who is a descendant of those who know of "U" is born without the knowledge of the BRAHMAN.**

Remember that the pervasiveness and fulfilling of the desires relate to physical and mental bodies. Therefore all that was completely covered in the previous aphorism belongs to the stage of Vaiśvānara. After we have achieved the state of Vaiśvānara or having resonated with the first syllable A of AUM, what exists?

Our contemplation will either automatically (divine race) or wilfully (human effort) shift from "A" to

"M" of the AUM. This leads us to becoming Taijasa and as we have already seen Taijasa is finer, subtler and superior in terms of its degree of closeness to the kingdom of God. How so? Taijasa was said to be the state of a dreamy or hazy state of consciousness. This relates to the Paśyaṃtī Vāk or the plant kingdom stage of evolution. But the glory of this Taijasa lies in it being the vault of root-principles. The physical and mental aspects sprout out of these root principles. We have already seen this earlier.

It seems that the "U" forms a fulcrum between the "A" and "M". That means when we slowly meditate on the second syllable, of course only after having mastered the state of "A", it makes us enter into the world of root principles. For example, gravity as a physical law is known by us in terms of the physical sight of a stone falling from a height and in terms of a thought of the same. This corresponds to the Gravity of Vaiśvānara. But when we meditate on "U" and enter into the Taijasa world, we will enter into the world of experience where we become Gravity i.e., we are the root principle of gravity. Then, instead of Newtnian laws of Relativistic laws which describe gravity in terms of known mathematics, we will understand it as a particular ray of divine plan emanating from GOD. The same is true with anything in this Universe and its root principle. This is better understood when we play chess or some puzzles. When we are involved in chess, we see that we move a piece even without our WILL acting (i.e., without our knowledge) and then we find ourselves at an advantage! This is because in that scenario, we have entered into the world of principles and that leads and steers the physical mind and hand in moving the chess piece. The degree of entrance into this Taijasic state makes all the difference between a winner and a loser. If you ask a chess champion how he knew the best move, the answer would be that he had already foresaw the opponent's moves upto certain degree. But if you again ask him how he saw that, the answer would be a blank. Because, even he does not know that he had entered the state of Taijasa where the opponent's moves were redunandly visible to his inner mind (higher pole) due to him becoming the very principle of chess! But because paśyaṃtī state is not comprehensible to the madhyamā or vaikharī (and that is why it is called dreamy/hazy) the winner does not know any such events happening in his inner self.

But the MU says that when we meditate on "U", we enter and we will start to condense the awareness of Taijasa. Previously in the case of the winner of chess, he could not condense the hidden developments. But because we already mastered "A" in the process of AUM, we went beyond the physical and mental by way of progress. Therefore, we are aware consciously of this dreamy or Paśyaṃtī state. This helps us to consciously understand the root principles of this creation one by one. Finally, we will become the root of all the root principles and hence we become the measure of all the laws of creation. This is what is called as "**Sa+Māna+Jñāna+Saṃtati**" = *The true measure of acquiring all the knowledge.* Here Jñāna implies the knowledge of root principles and not mere information. The latter belongs to physical/mental and the former to the beyondness.

It seems that there won't be any descendents of those who know this "U" who does not know Brahman. Why did the seers not keep it simple and say - "Those who know this 'U' will have a lineage of people who know Brahman?". There is a hidden import here. The "**Kula**" word does not imply physical descendents at all! This is because we are speaking of Taijasa which itself is not a physical entity. Therefore the Kula here implies the group-consciousness. KULA in sanskrit actually means a group of elements sharing common properties. Because the treatise of MU relates to the evolution of consciousness, Kula implies the notion of group-consciousness. Group-consciousness in this context means to be conscious of all the groups of principles governing the world of Vaiśvānara.

The aphorism would now mean that ***there won't be any person who has reached the stage of a group consciousness and yet does not know Brahman.*** But then, why use two negative remarks ? It is to suggest that even though a person has reached the stage of group-consciousness, he is still in the process of knowing and becoming Brahman and did not actually become Brahman yet. This is like a cautionary statement. Sometimes in the process of meditation, we tend to fool ourselves that we have reached the final stage of realizing Brahman due to the increased knowledge that we gain by entering and mastering the world of root principles. We need to be aware that this is only the second state - "U" and not the final Brahman stage and we need to humbly proceed without any self attributed fascinations! That is why they used two negatives for us to stop, think, analyze and put the essence into the synthesis of our approach.

∞∞∞

11. Syllable M - Prajña

Suṣuptasthānaḥ Prājñō Makārastṛtīyā Mātrā Mitērapītērvā Minōti Ha Vā Idaṃ Sarvamapītiśca Bhavati Ya Evaṁ Veda.

Word To Word Meaning:

Suṣuptasthānaḥ = *the realm of deep-sleep state;* **Prajñaḥ** = *the conscious-intelligence;* **Makāraḥ** = *the M;* **Tṛtīyā+Mātrā** = *the third mode of utterance;* **Mitēḥ** = *being the measure;* **Apītēḥ** = *and being the final;* **Vā** = *who;* **Minōti** = *measures;* **Ha Vai** = *certainly;* **Idaṃ** = *this;* **Sarvaṃ** = *all;* **Apītiḥ** = *dissolved;* **Ca** = *and;* **Bhavati** - *happens;* **Yaḥ** = *who;* **Ēvaṃ** = *thus;* **Vēda** = *knows.*

Import:

The third mode of utterance M is the conscious-intelligence belonging to the realm of deep-sleep state. It is the final measure of all that can be measured. Those who know this M will certainly enter this world of final-

measures and be dissolved in it.

Explanation:

The key points pertaining to the state of "M" are being described now.

- **Prajña is the "M".**
- **HE (M) is in a deep-sleep state.**
- **This "M" forms the final measure (of all measures).**
- **Those who know "M" will therefore, enter and exists beyond any measures**

When we utter AUM, the ending sound is that of the closing of lips as literal "M". But when we master the physical "A" of AUM, the "M" we utter becomes the sublime basis of sound which is the nasal "M". Here lips have no role but the breath in the nose and throat plays a role in uttering the "M". So this shows the role of subtler forces at play. When we master the "U" of AUM, we are taken into the world of true "M" which is beyond the audible sound "M". This is called "Nāda". Until previous stages, you at least tried to utter. But in this stage, your WILL dissolves and the utterance alone exists. That is why this is called a deep-sleep state or suṣupti or parā vāk or Prajña.

Nāda is said to be the body of the all-auspicious Brahman (Nāda Tanumniśaṃ) by saint Tyagaraja in one of his songs. That means the incomprehensible Brahman shines forth through the Nāda. Nādōpāsana is the upāsana or practice of meditating on the Nāda.

Note an interesting point here:

1. The "A" - belonged to Vaiśvānara who is the physical and mental world of creation. This is the way of **Rig Vēda**. ***Vāgēva Rigvēdaḥ*** says the Upaniṣads which means that the uttered word (and hence implicitly its meaning) is Rig Vēda.
2. The "U" belonged to Tijasa which is the inner-higher pole of the mind in creation. This is the way of Yajur Vēda. ***Manō Yajurvēdaḥ*** says the Upaniṣads which means that the mind (the true mind and hence the higher mind is inferred) is Yajur Vēda.
3. The "M" belongs to the Prajña which is the Nāda in creation. This is the way of **Sāma Vēda**. ***Prāṇaḥ Sāmavēdaḥ*** says the Upaniṣads which means that the Prāṇaḥ (prāṇa is the life or the music of periodical breath, which is but Nāda) is Sāma Vēda.

So the three aphorisms pertaining to A-U-M and the related practices conceal the essence of the Rig-Yajus-Sāma Vēdas.

Coming back, know that the act of meditating on Nāda is not in our jurisdiction at all. Remember it is equivalent to Parā state. Therefore, we enter into the meditative state of Nāda only after mastering the physical, mental and subtle worlds in us. Allegorically speaking, in this stage of "M", we experience the music of creation as coming from the strings of the musical instrument Vīṇā of the goddess of flow of consciousness - Saraswathi. Saraswathi means the flow of a running lake. Here, the lake is filled with consciousness as she is said to be the daughter-wife of creator consciousness (Brahma). She is a daughter by virtue of being the WORD created by Brahma and she is his wife because she is inseparable from the source due to eternal utterance! The instrument Vīṇa is symbolical to our head-spine system where the strings are the many Nāḍīs. Nāḍīs are channels through which different grades of energy flow - energy of sight, smell, digestion, reproduction,etc. So meditating on the Nāda is nothing but meditating on the vibratory flow of energy in the Nāḍīs and regulating it. In fact this is the essence of Kunḍalinī Yōgā and the Tantric ways of worshipping. But saints like Meerabai, Kabir das and Tyagaraja have shown that to enter into the world of Nāda is very easy through Bhakti or devotion. Bhakti truly implies a stage where a devotee offers himself i.e., the "I am"-ness is completely dissolved. Is this not the stage of Parā or Prajña as we have already explored? So, when we end at the meditation of "U" as the higher mind, it is dissolved and opens the door of Nāda ("M") to consciousness.

It seems that "M" is the measure of all measures and those who know this "M" will be dissolved as one with the final measure and hence stand beyond any measured measure. In the previous stage of "U" we became the measure of all the laws of creation. That means the laws still exist to us and hence we became their measures. When we transcend the stage of "U", the laws of creation no longer constrain us by their presence but instead dissolve in the deep-sleep state and hence cease to exist. Then the meaning to the measure of laws of creation also ceases to exist. What remains? Measure alone remains. This is called the source-measure or the mother-measure represented by the word - "**Mā**". In Sanskrit **Mā** means our birth-mother as well as the source-measure. What does it measure? It measures the measurement itself - meaning, from this "M" the concept of measurement arises and from this concept, the measurements of laws of creation arise and from them, the laws of creation themselves arise. That is why it is said to be the final-measure - no more measures, not even of itself, beyond this stage, can be made. That is why those who know "M" are beyond any measures!

∞∞∞

12. The Divine Essence Of Om Is Brahman

Amātraścaturthōvyavahāryaḥ Prapañcōpaśamaḥ Śivōdvaita Ēvamōṃkāra Ātmaiva Saṃviśatyāt-manātmānaṃ Ya Ēvaṃ Vēda Ya Ēvaṃ Vēda.

Word To Word Meaning:

A+Mātraḥ = *is not a mode of utterance;* Ca = *and;* Caturthaḥ = *the fourth part;* Avyavahāryaḥ = *cannot be spoken about;* Prapañca = *the world woven from five elements;* Upaśamaḥ = *ceases to exist;* Śivaḥ = *the auspicious;* Advaitaḥ = *non-dual;* Ēvaṃ = *thus;* Ōṃkāra = *AUM;* Ātmaiva = *the one soul;* Saṃviśati = *enters into;* Ātmanā = *by the (individual) soul;* Ātmānaṃ = *into the (Universal) soul;* Yaḥ = *who;* Ēvaṃ = *thus;* Vēda = *knows;* Yaḥ = *who;* Ēvaṃ = *thus;* Vēda = *knows.*

Import:

The fourth part is not a mode of utterance at all and it

cannot be spoken about. The world made of five elements ceases to exist (or dissolves in this). It is auspicious and non-dual. Those who know this, in fact those who know this alone, can enter into the Universal self from the individual self!

Explanation:

Thus, by mastering the "M" or the Nāda the consciousness becomes something that cannot be measured. As we have already seen any *adjective* is in one way or another a *measure.* We have also seen that BRAHMAN can not be measured. So, it was indirectly suggested before that those who master the "M" will enter into the world of Brahman which has no qualities!

VAIŚHVĀNARA	TAIJASA	PRAJÑA
A	U	M
Wakeful	Dreamy	Deep Sleep
Outward Consciousness	Inward Consciousness	Resonant Consciousness
Humans & Animals	Plants	Minerals
Jāgrt {lower & higher}	Svapna	Suṣupti
Vaikharī & Madhyamā	Paśyantī	Parā
7 gross limbs	7 subtle limbs	Itself
19 gross limbs	19 subtle limbs	Itself
Rig vēda	Yajurvēda	Sāmavēda

ŌM — AUM
Advaita — Non-Dual

The present aphorism indicates the culmination of the meditative approach of AUM. The key points are:

- **Nothing can be spoken about this stage**
- **The world of 5-elements cease to exist**
- **The absolute GOOD alone exists**
- **AUM is verily the Ātma**
- **The one who knows this enters the world of SELF beyond the dualities!**

This is the kingdom of GOD. If someone asks what is the purpose of this AUM-meditation, we can now safely say that the purpose is to enter into the kingdom of GOD. That is what MU proclaims! This kingdom, as has been seen earlier, can be described only in negative or double negative terms. But the word Śivaṃ, a positive term is used. How? Vēda says that the good and bad in human terms both put together is the absolute GOOD that a seer received. And a seer often speaks from the kingdom of GOD (i.e., BRAHMAN speaks through him or we say his utterance is from a realized state). Therefore, Śivaṃ actually implies the GOOD that exists beyond the relative good and bad. The 5-fold world exists only until duality exists. When duality ceases to exist, the world of 5-elements (physical, subtle, subtler as well as subtlest) vanishes. This is what is meant by the ceasing of Prapañca - all the worlds.

Next the MU says that AUM, which we have uttered

until now, as a separate entity from us, becomes verily us i.e., the utterance is also dissolved and the background ĀTMA alone shines. There is no layer of dualit to cover it. Ātma is equivalent to Brahman as has been established by us before. Therefore, AUM is verily Brahman. Remember the AUM uttered by us is different from the Brahman equivalent AUM that is being spoken here. AUM we uttered is our bi-product. But the cause of its utterance as well as the medium in which it is uttered is the actual AUM which is BRAHMAN. This is a fact to become rather than a fat to know.

Thus when we become the ĀTMA, there is nothing else to evolve and hence we have reached the culmination as well as the origin of creation. This is called the NON-DUALITY or ADVAITA - the first and the last stage of any creation or created entity.

This concludes the treatise of AUM by MU.

∞∞∞

Transliteration Scheme

Sanskrit- (vowels)	Transliteration	Pronunciation
अ	a	umbrella
आ	ā	father
इ	i	in
ई	ī	eat
उ	u	put
ऊ	ū	cool
ऋ	ṛ	christmas
ए	e, ē (elongated)	say
ऐ	ai	tie
ओ	o, ō (elongated)	no
औ	au	shout
◌ं	ṃ	sum
◌ः	ḥ	husk

Sanskrit (consonants)	Transliteration	Pronunciation
क	ka	crac**k**
ख	kha	**kha**ki
ग	ga	**g**um
घ	gha	a**gha**st
ङ	ṅa	p**unc**ture
च	ca	**cha**plin
छ	cha	**cha**mpion
ज	ja	**ju**mp
झ	jha	**jha**rkhand
ञ	ña	on**io**n
ट	ṭa	**t**urn
ठ	ṭha	-
ड	ḍa	**dou**ble
ढ	ḍha	a**dh**ere
ण	ṇa	-
ळ	ḷa	-

Sanskrit (consonants)	Transliteration	Pronunciation
त	ta	Math
थ	tha	thought
द	da	That
ध	dha	Dharma
न	na	Nine
प	pa	put
फ	pha	sphere
ब	ba	bunty
भ	bha	abhor
म	ma	mother
य	ya	yawn
र	ra	run
ल	la	laugh
व	va	want
श	ṣa	Shoulder
ष	śa	-
स	sa	sun
ह	ha	her

Acknowledgement

I am extremely grateful to my loving wife Lakshmi Deepika in bringing beauty to this book through her skilful art.

About The Author

Tejaswi Katravulapally

I hail from the pearl city of Hyderabad. I pursued B. Tech in ECE from LNMIIT, Jaipur and M.Sc. in Physics from IIT Madras. Later on I pursued a research career in the field of Quantum Physics. My research was funded by the European Union's prestigious scholarship scheme EMJD-EXTATIC. This led me to a successful completion of a joint doctoral degree (PhD) from Dublin City University, Ireland and Military University of Technology, Poland. My scientific research has been published in some of the most reputed academic physics journals such as Physical Review A, Atoms, etc.

Having brought up in a traditional Indian family environment, I have also developed a keen interest in the study of ancient scriptures. The years of my exploration resulted in the evolution of my spiritual outlook. I always study the ancient scriptures in the light of modern science and vice versa. I am an ardent disciple of Master E.K. Along with his works, I also follow the works of Sri Aurobindo, Sir John Woodroffe, H.P.Blavatsky, Alice A. Bailey, Swami Vivekananda, etc. Many ideologies have shaped my thought process over the time and helped me peek into the wide vistas of ancient's intuition. The outcomes of my spiritual explorations are regularly recorded in my blog - https://ardentdisciple.wordpress.com. I have authored two books titled Lalitā Priyadīpikā - a commentary to first 111 names of lalitā sahasraṇama, and Journey through the Vēdic thought - a commentary to 16 hymns of Puruṣa Sūkta of Rig Vēda. Paperback versions of both these books are available via Notion Press publishers. I have also authored a few interesting articles which found their place in some of the esteemed magazines of India.

You can contact me any time at ardentdisciple7@gmail.com.

Books By This Author

Journey Through The Vēdic Thought: An Exploration Of Puruṣa Sūktaṃ

Vēdic lore is one of the magnificent wisdom branches amongst the ancient ones. The thought process of a Vēdic seer is often non-linear and hence creates hurdles for the present day truth seeking explorers. The goal of this book is to help such an explorer with the process of attuning to the way of the Vēda. To this end, we will be taking the most famous hymn of Puruṣa Sūktaṃ of the Rig Vēdic text and try to understand the perspective of the Vēdic principles by decoding the depths of this hymn.

Only after understanding the basic bricks of the Vēda, can one enter into its specific contents. So, a solid introduction is given at the start, which helps the reader to attune their contemplative attitude to that of the Vēdic seers. The introductory part covers the topics such as - What is Vēda? What is the difference between a Vēda and a Vēdic text? How many Vēdās are there and why? What do we mean by Chandas? How did Vēdic hymns come into existence at all? What does it mean by the Vēda is eternal? etc. After such a serious ride into the deep canals of the Vēdic foundations, we enter into the topic of the hymn itself. It consists of 16 stanzas in total. A word to word meaning, an import and a thorough explanation is given for each of the hymns. Where necessary, some diagrams were also given to convey the key points of the stanzas to the reader.

What is the difference between this book and the existing works on Puruṣa Sukta? The main differences are the approach and the goal. The approach that I took for this book is that of a unified outlook. The unification is in terms of Physics, Vēda, Upaniṣads, Esoteric, Occult, Purāṇās, Etymology, Astrology, etc. The goal is not to understand Puruṣa Sūktaṃ as an individual literary piece, but to understand it as a torch that shines upon the Vēdic thought process. It is simple to give meaning to the hymns by using a dictionary. But it is a tough job to see and bring out a harmonious picture of the hymn in relation to the ancient Vēdic thought. After reading this book, the reader is sure to get a correct orientation towards understanding the Vēda, exactly as intended by the Vēdic seers.

Lalitā Priyadīpikā: Splendours Of The World Mother (Vol. 1)

In the ancient lore that flourished in the land of Bhārat (India), there is one particular branch of wisdom which lived through the test of time. That is the worshipping of the lord through the thousand names. This is called by the name "Sahasranāma". "Sahasra" means thousand or infinite and "Nāma" means a name. To worship the lord with thousand names means to utter each name through the vocals and meditate on its meaning. It is the proclamation of this wisdom branch that such a meditation can dissolve one's individual self in the universal self of the ONE Omniness.

Splendors of that Omniscient lord are often addressed as the "World Mother or Lalitā". Lalitā Sahasranāma are the thousand names that address the many qualities of the world mother and helps an aspirant who wishes to experience the splendors of the almighty.

This series "Lalitā Priyadīpika" is an attempt to explore the nature of all the thousand names that are found in the original text of Lalitā Sahasranāma. The exploration will be in considerable depth. Word-to-word meaning of each of the names are given along with an explanation of the hymn containing the name and a detailed exposition of the manifold nature of the meaning of the name. This is done thorugh the synthesis of many branches of wisdom. Only such a harmonious synthesis can lead to blissful understanding of hiden mysteries of creation as explored in ancient scriptures.

For Volume-1, 1-51 names are taken and explored. Volume-2 having names from 52-111 is ready and will be published soon. Further volumes are planned to expound on remainng names. The reason to choose first 111 names is that these 111 names, in quintessence, capture the most important aspects of the whole text of Lalitā Sahasranāma.

Reader is gently asked to note that for the source names, which are in Sanskrit, IAST (International Alphabet of Sanskrit Transliteration) scheme is used.

Lalitā Priyadīpikā: Splendours Of The World Mother (Vol. 2)

In the ancient lore that flourished in the land of Bhārat (India), there is one particular branch of wisdom which lived through the test of time. That is the worshipping of the lord through the thousand names. This is called by the name "Sahasranāma". "Sahasra" means thousand or infinite and "Nāma" means a name. To worship the lord with thousand names means to utter each name through the vocals and meditate on its meaning. It is the proclamation of this wisdom branch that such a meditation can dissolve one's individual self in the universal self of the ONE Omniness.

Splendors of that Omniscient lord are often addressed as the "World Mother or Lalitā". Lalitā Sahasranāma are the thousand names that address the many qualities of the world mother and helps an aspirant who wishes to experience the splendors of the almighty.

This series "Lalitā Priyadīpika" is an attempt to explore the nature of all the thousand names that are found in the original text of Lalitā Sahasranāma. The exploration will be in considerable depth. Word-to-word meaning of each of the names are given along with an explanation of the hymn containing the name and a detailed exposition of the manifold nature of the meaning of the name. This is done thorugh the synthesis of many branches of wisdom. Only such a harmonious synthesis can lead to blissful understanding of hiden mysteries of creation as explored in ancient scriptures.

For Volume-1, 1-51 names were taken and explored. The present Volume-2 having names from 52-111. Further volumes are planned to expound on remainng names. The reason to choose first 111 names is that these 111 names, in quintessence, capture the most important aspects of the whole text of Lalitā Sahasranāma.

Reader is gently asked to note that for the source

names, which are in Sanskrit, IAST (International Alphabet of Sanskrit Transliteration) scheme is used.

Printed in Great Britain
by Amazon

25934200R00069